Writing About Literature

B. Bernard Cohen
WICHITA STATE UNIVERSITY

Scott, Foresman and Company
CHICAGO   ATLANTA   DALLAS   PALO ALTO   FAIR LAWN, N.J.

PREFACE

This book is the outgrowth of many years of teaching experience in colleges and universities located in different geographical areas of the United States and dedicated to differing educational objectives, ranging from technical to general education, from teacher training to liberal arts. In all of these institutions, I have found that at some point during the freshman or sophomore year teachers ask students to write essays on literature. Frequently a whole course is devoted to an introduction to literature, with interpretative papers required. In teaching such courses, I have discovered many books which deal with composition in general and numerous ones which introduce the student to the reading of literature. But I have not encountered any text which discusses fully the relationships between reading and writing about literature or any book which stresses the student's specific problems in writing papers analyzing literary works. At almost every level of the college experience, I have found students who possess valuable insight into literature but who do not understand how to channel that insight into well-organized and effective essays on the literary work they are examining.

To assist these students, most of this book deals with the practical problems they will encounter in writing essays—for this reason, it has been entitled *Writing About Literature*. However, because I believe that the reading process is inseparable from the writing process, I have felt it necessary to include a first chapter, "A Pre-Writing Primer," which reviews certain basic principles, approaches, and attitudes to help make the students' analytical reading successful. This chapter stresses such problems as the difference between literal and analytical reading, the importance of context, the relevance of figurative language to analysis, and the validity of multiple interpretation of a work. I emphasize tech-

L. C. Number 63-15766

niques such as the use of symbolism in literature and the structure of poetry and fiction. To meet the student's frequent complaint that he cannot detect symbols, I have provided a series of questions designed to lead him to symbolical reading.

This chapter should be supplemented by the Glossary and the Suggestions for Analyzing Literature. The Glossary makes cross references to those terms which have been previously discussed and treats fully those which require further elaboration. Not only do I define the terms, but I also relate them to the process of analytical reading. I hope that the treatment in Chapter 1, the Glossary, and the Suggestions for Analyzing Literature will synthesize the tools of analysis and emphasize discipline which will help the student in approaching the writing process.

The major portion of the book, however, is concerned with the practical problems a student meets in attempting to write an essay on a literary work: development of a theme idea, solidity of content, organization of an essay, and matters of style. It is this feature that I feel is unique and that I hope will prove most helpful. The problems treated are derived from classroom experience and are frequently illustrated by students' work. I attempt to make the illustrations meaningful by analyzing them in terms of the principle or problem which they demonstrate. Wherever possible, I provide models of good interpretation or procedure.

In the appendices I have also placed a theme-grading chart whose symbols will allow the teacher to pinpoint basic principles when he grades his students' essays. At the same time, the use of the chart can become an important part of the student's learning process. By reviewing in the book the problems called to his attention, he has the opportunity to recognize them clearly and hence to avoid them in future papers.

In addition to providing guidance for reading literature and writing interpretative essays, I have included a final chapter which introduces research as a means of literary analysis. Here the assumption is that one cannot always write about literature out of the context of an author's life, his times, the traditions he follows or alters, or the body of criticism stimulated by his work. To illustrate this assumption, I have selected and discussed three ways to relate research and interpretation: the relationship of biography to interpretation, the examination of criticism of a given work, and the exploration of the creative process as a means of determining an author's intention.

Since this book can be used in conjunction with any anthology or group of texts chosen by the teacher, I have tried to keep *Writing About Literature* reasonably self-contained. A group of literary works has been carefully selected for illustrations and analysis. The student who wishes to use the book properly should therefore first read all of the poems and stories included, especially "The Ambitious Guest," "Flowering Judas," and "Old Mr. Marblehall," reprinted at the end of the book. It has been impossible, however, to keep the book entirely self-contained. In order to relieve the monotony of repeatedly citing a few works, I have occasionally referred to some plays, stories, or novels which are not reprinted here but which represent eminent literary works that are widely available. Even a student without previous acquaintance with these should be able to understand the principles they illustrate in the text. In addition, such works might provide a valuable supplemental reading list. The foremost of these references are Sophocles' *Oedipus the King;* Shakespeare's *Hamlet, Macbeth,* and *The Tempest;* Melville's *Moby Dick;* Twain's *Huckleberry Finn;* Lardner's "Haircut"; Miller's *Death of a Salesman;* and Salinger's *The Catcher in the Rye.*

I wish to thank Walter Merrill, chairman of the English Department of Wichita State University, for making possible a mimeographed version of this text for use in classes; James B. Haman of the Georgia Institute of Technology for a searching and valuable analysis of that version; and the editorial staff of Scott, Foresman and Company for numerous helpful suggestions. I am also grateful to the many students who have contributed to this volume. I refer not only to the examples which their themes have provided but also to the enrichment of my own experience gained through the many attempts which they and I have made to define and diagnose their problems and their strengths in the writing of literary interpretations.

Through every stage of the development of this book my wife, Lucian, has worked with me. She has offered not only encouragement but also skillful and professional criticism of the manuscript.

TABLE OF CONTENTS

Chapter 1

A PRE-WRITING PRIMER

If one attempts to write an interpretation of a literary work without reading and analyzing it carefully, he is likely to produce a poor essay. What he knows and what he does before he even tries to write his first draft is crucial. Therefore, the purpose of this chapter is to provide the student with some fundamental principles and information about the reading and interpreting of a literary work so that he can come to the writing process with something worth-while to say. Although works representing specific classifications of literature will be used as examples, the principles they illustrate are in most cases applicable to the analysis of three major types — fiction (short stories and novels), poetry, and drama.

LITERAL VERSUS ANALYTICAL READING

Analytical reading, another name for interpretation, differs from literal reading in that it requires closer attention to the suggestive power of words, the relationships of details, and the totality of meaning that emerges from them. The student of literature should recognize that he cannot write a good essay on a poem or a story by relying on its literal meaning. If he depends solely on dictionary definitions, on paraphrase, and on summary, his approach will be literal and inadequate. If he can progress from denotation to connotation, and from summary to analysis, he will find richer material for interpretative essays.

Denotation Versus Connotation. In the beginning, one should comprehend the precise meaning of the words in a text under consideration. Denotation is the dictionary definition or the exact meaning of a word as one can best determine it. In the poem "The Heavy Bear Who Goes with Me," reprinted below, the denotative meaning of the animal is extremely important.

The Heavy Bear Who Goes with Me[1]

"the withness of the body" —— Whitehead

The heavy bear who goes with me,
A manifold honey to smear his face,
Clumsy and lumbering here and there,
The central ton of every place,
The hungry beating brutish one
In love with candy, anger, and sleep,
Crazy factotum, dishevelling all,
Climbs the building, kicks the football,
Boxes his brother in the hate-ridden city.

Breathing at my side, that heavy animal,
That heavy bear who sleeps with me,
Howls in his sleep for a world of sugar,
A sweetness intimate as the water's clasp,
Howls in his sleep because the tight-rope
Trembles and shows the darkness beneath.
— The strutting show-off is terrified,
Dressed in his dress-suit, bulging his pants,
Trembles to think that his quivering meat
Must finally wince to nothing at all.

That inescapable animal walks with me,
Has followed me since the black womb held,
Moves where I move, distorting my gesture,
A caricature, a swollen shadow,
A stupid clown of the spirit's motive,
Perplexes and affronts with his own darkness,
The secret life of belly and bone,
Opaque, too near, my private, yet unknown,
Stretches to embrace the very dear
With whom I would walk without him near,
Touches her grossly, although a word
Would bare my heart and make me clear,

1. From *In Dreams Begin Responsibilities* by Delmore Schwartz. Copyright 1938 by New Directions and reprinted by their permission.

Stumbles, flounders, and strives to be fed
Dragging me with him in his mouthing care,
Amid the hundred million of his kind,
The scrimmage of appetite everywhere.

Delmore Schwartz

A bear has observable physical characteristics and habits. Since these can be examined scientifically, the word that stands for the animal has a normally well-defined denotation. In the poem some of the denotative qualities of the bear are present: a bear is large, tends to be clumsy, and is fond of honey.

Yet a close reader of the poem will observe that other activities are associated with the bear which are not part of a denotative meaning of the word. A bear does not ordinarily climb buildings, kick footballs, or box his brothers "in the hate-ridden city." Nor does a bear sleep with people. The definition of the bear can no longer be confined to dictionary or scientific descriptions.

Connotation now becomes important and leads one away from a literal view of the bear. Connotation includes the implications and inferences of words, phrases, or figures of speech. An examination of the unusual activities of the bear relates them to man's inner feelings and drives—his hates and his lust. The bear is no longer a bear, but a symbol which provides a key to interpreting the poem as a conflict between man's appetites or urges and his sense of reason which counsels restraint. Therefore, although denotation provides a useful starting point, the connotations within a literary work must be pursued in order to reach an analytical interpretation.

Paraphrase and Summary Versus Analysis. Paraphrase and summary, like denotation, are tools of literal reading. A paraphrase in fact depends on dictionary definitions, for it is an attempt to translate the words of the literary work into more simple and understandable equivalents. If the work is a poem, a paraphrase is a prose rendition of it. As an example, let us paraphrase the first stanza of Poe's poem "To Helen," which follows:

Helen, thy beauty is to me
  Like those Nicéan barks of yore,
That gently, o'er a perfumed sea,
  The weary, way-worn wanderer bore
  To his own native shore.

> On desperate seas long wont to roam,
>   Thy hyacinth hair, thy classic face,
> Thy Naiad airs have brought me home
>   To the glory that was Greece,
>   And the grandeur that was Rome.
>
> Lo! in yon brilliant window-niche
>   How statue-like I see thee stand,
> The agate lamp within thy hand!
>   Ah, Psyche, from the regions which
>   Are Holy-Land!

A paraphrase of stanza one would read: "Helen, to me your beauty is like the ancient Nicéan ships that carried the tired wanderer comfortably over the sea to his homeland." This paraphrase has rendered words such as *barks of yore* into easier prose equivalents; it has changed the syntax or sentence structure of the stanza; it has also removed the musical quality and beauty of the language. Although accurate in its transcription, this paraphrase still has not provided much help toward interpreting the poem. The prose translation is too literal and in fact destroys the beauty of the original.

A summary would also confine one to a literal approach to stories, poems, and dramas. A summary is a condensation of a literary work — an attempt to present in as few words as possible its literal or surface meaning. A summary of the entire poem "To Helen" might be: "Helen's beauty has comforted me and led me securely home." Anyone who offers this summary as an interpretation has not begun to penetrate the poem; he is merely reading it literally and minimally.

A summary of a story or a plot is sometimes referred to as a synopsis. The following synopsis of "The Ambitious Guest" (pp. 159-166) is as inadequate as the summary of "To Helen":

> A stranger who is driven by an overwhelming ambition to acquire renown stops overnight with a family in the mountains. During his conversation with the family, each member of the group expresses a wish. After the grandmother reveals her desire, a mountain slide occurs, and everyone rushes to the barrier constructed for such emergencies. The slide divides, leaving the house standing intact, but destroying both the barrier and all the people, whose bodies are never discovered.

Such a synopsis condenses the action occurring in the story, but it does not reveal the meaning the author sought to convey through the events. Hence it does not probe beneath the simple surface of the story.

In order to interpret literature, one must analyze it. Seeking denotative meanings and using paraphrase and summary are first steps toward analysis, but in themselves, they are inadequate substitutes for interpretation. Analysis involves many aspects of literary study: an understanding of context and the logical relationships between words and details in a poem or story; a comprehension of imagery, which is basic to figurative reading; an awareness of the totality or structure of a literary work; and a concentration on the techniques of an author as a way of determining his meanings or purposes.

CONTEXT AND ANALYSIS

All intelligent analysis and interpretation is based on a careful study of context, the surroundings in which an element of a literary work appears. These elements may be words, phrases, sentences, paragraphs, images, allusions, or plot details. In narrative or in drama there are also contexts for people and their actions: the settings or environments in which they live, the events which surround them, and the other people who enter their lives. Ideas also have contexts — people whose actions represent them, meaningful events, or the key words and sentences the author uses to express his concepts.

The allusions in the poem "To Helen" demonstrate graphically the importance of context in analytical and figurative reading. An allusion is a reference, real or fictional, to someone, some event, or something in the Bible, history, literature, or any phase of culture. The reference will have an original meaning, but it must be studied in the context of the literary work in which it appears.

The lazy reader of "To Helen" will insist that it is merely a tribute to a beautiful woman and hence will not bother to check the allusions in the poem unless he is using a book with explanatory footnotes. Yet these allusions would lead the careful reader away from the literal level to a satisfactory interpretation of the poem. For example, the adjective *hyacinth* describing Helen's hair alludes to Hyacinth, whom the god Apollo changed into the flower bearing his name. In classical mythology a *Naiad* is a nymph of lakes, rivers, and fountains. Thus Helen is put in the context of the supernatural. Although there is much controversy about the meaning of *Nicéan barks,* most students relate the phrase either to Greek or Roman literary sources. The reference to *Psyche* fuses the Homeric myth of Helen of Troy with that of Psyche, who loved Cupid devotedly and who is a traditional symbol of the soul. All of these allusions clearly link the Helen of the poem to classical literature and mythology. On the other hand, *Holy-Land* seems to introduce a Christian spirituality.

From what point of view do these allusions come? The perceptive reader will notice that the poem is narrated, perhaps by the poet. The narrator is linked to Helen; that is, her attraction is irresistible to him. The words associated with Helen stress her beauty; those referring to the narrator indicate turmoil ("weary, way-worn wanderer" roaming over "desperate seas"). Thus Helen's beauty seems to contrast with the narrator's pain, yet at the same time her beauty comforts him.

The careful reader will attempt to investigate the nature of this attraction to Helen. At this point what he knows about the allusions will begin to fit into a pattern of interpretation. He may try to get at the problem by examining the way in which the interpretation of Helen's beauty builds up. Each stanza emphasizes beauty beyond her literal physical beauty. In the first stanza, the reference to "weary, way-worn wanderer" (perhaps Ulysses) associates Helen and the narrator of the poem with the classical epics of Homer—that is, with the legendary beauty of Helen. In the second stanza, through the allusions and the last two lines, her beauty is linked to the entire classical culture, not only of Greece but also of Rome. In the third stanza, Helen becomes equated with soul (Psyche) and Holy-Land; hence she is spiritual beauty, both pagan and Christian. Through the progression of the stanzas, Poe develops for the perceptive reader a climactic description of the beauty that goes beyond the face and figure of a woman.

Thus, to say that the poem is merely about a beautiful woman is to miss the relationships between the allusions and the progression of the stanzas, and between the narrator, the poet, and his subject, Helen. To the poet, Helen's beauty is three-fold: it embodies Homeric legend, the Greek and Roman culture, and classical-Christian spirituality.

Fitted into context, the allusions function meaningfully within the poem. Other relationships within the poem have also contributed to the interpretation. The words describing the *I,* the narrator, and those depicting Helen have been put together so that both the contrast and the close relationship between them can be determined. The associations surrounding the name Helen, another allusion to a definite woman in myth and literature, have been considerably expanded until she becomes representative of spiritual beauty.

Other examples of the importance of context to analysis can be cited. In "The Heavy Bear," the meaning of the word *bear* can be arrived at only by putting together *all* of the animal's actions. In "The Ambitious Guest," the stranger's ambition must be put in the context of the humble wishes of the members of the family, and it must also be linked to the persistent emphasis on death in the story. If one were to examine the character of Braggioni in "Flowering Judas" (reprinted on pp. 167-178), he would have to bring together the various actions and words of the rebel leader; he would also have to examine those phrases and sentences which reveal Miss Porter's attitude toward the character before he could generalize about any of Braggioni's traits. (See CHARACTERIZATION in the Glossary.)

Awareness of context involves a logical process of relating details from which conclusions can be drawn. This process goes on at all times in literary analysis and helps one advance considerably beyond paraphrase and summary.

IMAGERY AND ANALYSIS

As we have already seen, the connotation of words can lead a reader beyond the literal surface of a story or poem to a more profound or figurative meaning. Figurative meaning can be defined as the understanding arrived at as a result of a study of connotations of words, images, and figures of speech. The term *imagery* can be used to include both images and figures of speech. These, of course, are meaningful in context, and sometimes similar images are so prevalent in a work that they form patterns.

The Image As a Direct Sense Impression. An image is a sense impression created by a sense appeal in words. Such an appeal should present a description so graphic that the reader can visualize what is being described and perhaps can associate it with his own experience. When in Sonnet 73 (see p. 52) Shakespeare refers to "yellow leaves, or none, or few" that hang upon the boughs of the trees, any reader who has experienced late autumn can picture the scene. The sunset fading in the west and the expiring fire are also definite visual images. In "The Heavy Bear," one can literally see the bear climbing a building, kicking a football, and boxing. Although all of these actions are within one's experience, he may normally not associate them with the bear. Despite this incongruity, the images created by Schwartz are quite clear. The first two stanzas of "La Belle Dame sans Merci" (reprinted on pp. 14-16) and much of the Knight's own narrative in the poem contain sense impressions of all kinds — for example, the withered sedge and the paleness and haggardness of the Knight.

In all these poems, however, the clear descriptive details which establish sense images become meaningful in context. In each case the images are relevant to man's condition — the empty tree is linked to dying, the bear's vigorous activity to man's emotions and instincts, and the withering sedge to the Knight's spiritual decline. Although an image can be strictly descriptive — that is, meaningful only for what it describes — the image in context frequently takes on figurative meaning in literature.

Figures of Speech. Figures of speech are images that are often deliberately indirect; they depend on a process of association, the forced linking of two elements. Among the many possible kinds of figures of speech, four are worth pointing to: the simile, personification, metaphor, and symbol. Although the simile and personification are not especially difficult, each broadens the meaning of any comparison. A simile makes a direct comparison between two elements and is usually introduced by *like* or *as.* In the poem "To Helen," Helen's beauty is "Like those Nicéan barks" which gently convey the "weary, way-worn wanderer" home. The comparison stresses the soothing and graceful effect of Helen. In Keats' sonnet "On First Looking into Chapman's Homer" (reprinted on p. 56), the last six lines or sestet contains two comparisons whereby Keats expands the importance of his experience in discovering Chapman's translation of Homer.

To demonstrate that prose writers also use figures of speech, we can cite several similes pertaining to Laura in "Flowering Judas." Laura's fear of Braggioni stifles her desire to flee "into the street where the houses lean together like conspirators under a single mottled lamp." Her real feelings suppressed, "she looks at Braggioni, frankly and clearly, like a good child who understands the rules of behavior." The two similes are appropriate, for in the conspiratorial environment of the revolution dominated by Braggioni, Laura is indeed a child who cannot exercise her will. Laura's response to the youth who courted her is also conveyed by a simile in the midst of a poetic passage:

> The moonlight spread a wash of gauzy silver over the clear spaces of the garden, and the shadows were cobalt blue. The scarlet blossoms of the Judas tree were dull purple, and the names of the colors repeated themselves automatically in her mind, while she watched not the boy, but his shadow, fallen like a dark garment across the fountain rim, trailing in the water.

The dark garment blankets the romantic colors of the scene and represents the failure of the youth's passionate courting. The futility of his love has earlier been described in the simile of his singing "like a lost soul." Ironically, the simile is also applicable to Laura, who wanders "like a lost soul" in the cynical maze of the revolution.

Personification (see ALLEGORY in the Glossary) is the giving of human characteristics or shape to an inanimate object, to an emotion or instinct, to a moral quality, to an event like death, or to an invisible essence like the soul. The coupling of inanimate with human elements forces the reader to associate two entities. An excellent example can be found in Sir Walter Raleigh's "The Lie," where the soul is personified as the spokesman protecting the poet's reputation. The first stanza follows:

> Go, soul, the body's guest,
>   Upon a thankless arrant [errand];
> Fear not to touch the best;
>   The truth shall be thy warrant.
>   Go, since I needs must die,
>   And give the world the lie.

A more modern instance of personification occurs in Emily Dickinson's poem "Because I could not stop for Death," where the author portrays Death as a gentleman caller who conveys her in a carriage to immortality.

Thus simile and personification automatically expand one's reading experience beyond the literal approach. Even more complex in figurative reading are metaphors and symbols. A metaphor is a direct or indirect substitution of one element for another. A passage from *Macbeth* (Act V, Scene v) demonstrates strikingly the importance of metaphor to figurative reading.

After Macbeth learns of his wife's death, he utters the famous
passage:

> She should have died hereafter;
> There would have been a time for such a word.
> To-morrow, and to-morrow, and to-morrow,
> Creeps in this petty pace from day to day
> To the last syllable of recorded time,
> And all our yesterdays have lighted fools
> The way to dusty death. Out, out, brief candle!
> Life's but a walking shadow, a poor player
> That struts and frets his hour upon the stage
> And then is heard no more: it is a tale
> Told by an idiot, full of sound and fury,
> Signifying nothing.

In this passage life is directly related to at least four elements which in effect substitute for life and graphically describe it: the "brief candle," "a walking shadow," "a poor player"
with his hour upon the stage, and "a tale told by an idiot." The
implications of the flickering and the snuffing out of the candle
refer to the brevity of man's existence. The metaphor of the
"walking shadow" has a double implication because the word
shadow looks back to the candle which casts its shadow, and the
word *walking* looks forward to the strutting player. The metaphor
of the player is linked to the candle by the brevity of his performance — the brevity of life. By implication the player's acting
("strutting and fretting") is man's span of life. The stage then
becomes the context of living. When the metaphor shifts to equate
life with a tale, the connection with the stage metaphors is clear.
The play, one would infer, has a story or plot and hence is a tale.
But the story or tale of man's life is told by an idiot. Although
there is much sound and fury in his incoherent babbling, there
is no worth-while result. Through this series of closely knit metaphors, most of which are the direct association of two elements,
Shakespeare portrays Macbeth's utter disillusionment about
the brevity and noisy emptiness of life.

Throughout the passage there is a vast image of time — an
implied metaphor whereby all phases of time are equated with
life. A close reader gets a distinct image of time — man's living
within the framework of time — being narrowed down to the
terminal point of death and nothingness. Starting with words
like *time* and *hereafter* connoting indefiniteness and vastness,
the reader comes to the more definite units of time measured in

days — the to-morrows (the future), the days (the present), the yesterdays (the past), and the "day to day" (a continuing movement). From these the reader goes to the four direct metaphors referred to. Time narrows down to the brevity of the existence of the candle and to the one hour upon the stage of life. Finally it comes to the nothingness of both life and death — Macbeth's destiny.

Although poetry generally relies more heavily on figures of speech, the same connotative use of language occurs in prose. In a passage in which she indicates that Braggioni will never die of his professional and profitable love of humanity, Miss Porter says, "He will live to see himself kicked out from his feeding trough by other hungry world-saviours." Although she is writing about human beings, the metaphors equate man and animals without directly associating them. A *feeding trough* is a long, open, narrow container from which animals obtain food or water, their nourishment to sustain life. With her emphasis on the verb *kicked out* and on the hunger of the other *world-saviours,* Miss Porter effectively establishes the bitter struggle for power among revolutionists in terms of the activities of animals, probably pigs. The metaphor reveals her ironic contempt for the professional and fraudulent revolutionist.

In either prose or poetry, then, the implications and relationships of the direct and implied metaphors that are employed by the author can contribute to a deeper understanding of the work and can, in addition, supply material for an interpretative essay.

SYMBOLISM AND ANALYSIS

The highest level of figurative reading involves symbols. The original meaning of the word *symbol* is a throwing together, a violent fusion, or the act of association. Indeed, a symbol is a process of association or fusion of two elements. The symbol itself usually begins with some concrete form — a physical condition, an object (animate or inanimate), or an event. In the context of a literary work, the concrete element suggests an abstract concept or meaning. Thus, through a careful study of the tangible item the reader is led to an understanding of the vital idea. In this way the concrete and the abstract fuse. The symbol is distinguished from the metaphor largely by degree: the symbol should be far more dominant in a poem or story than the metaphor. In effect, an extended metaphor might just as well be called a symbol.

Although symbols vary in complexity, one has to concentrate on the means whereby he can discover the concept or concepts suggested by the concrete element. Sometimes there will be a direct equation either because the author labels his symbol ("The gluttonous bulk of Braggioni has become a symbol of her [Laura's] many disillusions. . . .") or because the symbol has a generally accepted meaning (olive branch equals peace, for instance). Sometimes the symbol or structure of symbols depends on the use of an allusion which figures importantly in the context of the work. For example, the Judas tree calls forth the story of Judas and becomes applicable to Braggioni and Laura, especially in her dream. The tree associated with the betrayer of Christ ultimately becomes a symbol to explain how Braggioni has betrayed the ideals of the Mexican revolution. Another example would be the application of Homeric myths to the poem "To Helen."

Frequently a symbol grows directly out of the context of a work. For example, the bear in Schwartz' poem becomes a symbol only in terms of the specific activities and associations of the bear within the context of the poem. The same procedure operates in "La Belle Dame" (reprinted on pp. 14-16), in which the grot and the cold hill's side become symbols in context. At times one encounters a personal symbol created by an author. Writers like Blake, Yeats, and Faulkner, who have created their own mythologies, use personal symbols. In these cases one must often do research into the lives and works of the writers in order to understand the symbol. The research has to be applied to the work and studied in that context. Still another kind of symbol requires analysis from different points of view—the symbol of multiple perspective. In *Moby Dick* the whale does not mean the same thing to everybody. To Ahab the white whale is frequently associated with all of the evil heaped upon mankind since the fall of Adam. Yet to Ishmael the whiteness of the whale represents a mysterious and ambiguous coexistence of good and evil. Hence, a reader has to examine the reactions of each important character to the whale in order to determine the different meanings it represents.

Finally, a persistent pattern of metaphors and similes (a pattern of imagery) can become symbolical by the process of cumulative effect. In these cases careful relating of the images in their context would be the means of analysis. In *Macbeth* there are so many references to blood and to sleep or lack of sleep that they accumulate symbolical value. In *Oedipus the King* there are so many images of seeing and blindness that an ironical pattern of imagery is created. Seeing, in effect, becomes a symbol of mental blindness, and physical blindness becomes a symbol of knowledge and awareness.

Because students frequently complain that they cannot recognize symbols, the following questions which demonstrate some criteria for determining symbols should be carefully studied and applied to literary analysis:

1) Is the author directly equating an object or event with some abstract meaning? Is the equation of the two clear, though not labeled?

2) Does the emphasis upon highly connotative words suggest the necessity of symbolical reading?

3) Has the author introduced an allusion or a myth (the fall of Adam in the Garden of Eden, for instance) so strongly that it becomes symbolical in the context of the work? Has the context altered the original meaning of the allusion or myth? How?

4) What does the *immediate* context of a person, object, or event in a poem or story reveal about the possibility of symbolical reading? If in the *total* context any object or event is repeatedly referred to or has meaningful relationships with other details, is there room for symbolical reading?

5) Do the author's technical resources, such as characterization or his use of patterns of imagery, suggest symbols?

6) If the student knows other works by the same author, do these help interpret the symbolism of the particular work being analyzed?

7) Does the unusual or bizarre nature of the symbols suggest that they are private (personal to the author) and that research into biography or other areas must be done?

THE STRUCTURE AND TOTALITY OF A WORK AND ANALYSIS

An important way to transcend literal reading is to examine a literary work as a totality in terms of its structure. Too often the student will either ignore details in a poem or story or concentrate so much on the small pieces that he never observes the totality. By seeing how the various elements in a work function together, one can acquire much insight. Structure is the basic organization or arrangement of events, details, words, or parts (chapters, stanzas, scenes) in a literary work.

Structure of Poetry. The structure of poetry which does not contain a story can be examined through attention to:

1) Key words or repeated sentence patterns serving as meaningful threads
2) Dominant symbols or patterns of imagery
3) Stanzaic progression—the relationship of each stanza to the other
4) Logical progression, for example, cause-effect or question-answer
5) Conventional patterns based on the traditions of a type of poetry, for example, the structure of sonnets and rhyme schemes
6) The typography of the page—the poet's deliberate arrangement of words or even syllables into separate lines
7) A dominant theme or idea
8) A dominant emotion or mood
9) The author's tone, his attitude toward the material in the poem
10) Something nonpoetic, such as the jazz medium, imposed on poetic form
11) A psychological pattern
12) Any combination of these

In the poem "To Helen," we saw that the allusions and the central symbol, Helen, were related to the arrangement, or architecture, of the stanzas. "La Belle Dame" provides an excellent opportunity for structural analysis in which one can see the relationships among symbols, key words, devices of parallel structure, and patterns of imagery, all of which contribute to the totality or unity of the poem's structure. The text of the poem (original version) follows:

La Belle Dame sans Merci

I.

O what can ail thee, Knight at arms,
　Alone and palely loitering?
The sedge has withered from the Lake
　And no birds sing!

II.

5　O what can ail thee, Knight at arms,
　So haggard, and so woe begone?

The Squirrel's granary is full
    And the harvest's done.

III.

   I see a lily on thy brow
10   With anguish moist and fever dew,
And on thy cheeks a fading rose
    Fast withereth too —

IV.

I met a Lady in the Meads,
    Full beautiful, a faery's child
15 Her hair was long, her foot was light
    And her eyes were wild —

V.

I made a Garland for her head,
    And bracelets too, and fragrant Zone
She look'd at me as she did love
20   And made sweet moan —

VI.

I set her on my pacing steed
    And nothing else saw all day long
For sidelong would she bend and sing
    A faery's song —

VII.

25 She found me roots of relish sweet
    And honey wild and manna dew
And sure in language strange she said
    I love thee true —

VIII.

She took me to her elfin grot
30   And there she wept and sigh'd full sore,
And there I shut her wild wild eyes
    With kisses four.

IX.

And there she lulled me asleep
  And there I dream'd, Ah Woe betide!
35 The latest dream I ever dreamt
  On the cold hill side.

X.

I saw pale Kings, and Princes too
  Pale warriors, death pale were they all;
They cried, La belle dame sans merci
40 Thee hath in thrall.

XI.

I saw their starv'd lips in the gloam
  With horrid warning gaped wide,
And I awoke, and found me here
  On the cold hill's side.

XII.

45 And this is why I sojourn here
  Alone and palely loitering;
Though the sedge is withered from the Lake
  And no birds sing ——

               John Keats

    At first glance, the structure of the poem is based on a situation—a conversation between two speakers, comprising the questions of a stranger and the story of the Knight in response. In addition to this situational structure, there is a far more subtle organization of the poem established by many devices which correlate the theme and mood of the poem. The divisions of the two kinds of structure would look like this:

Situational Structure	*Thematic Structure*	

Questions
  Stanzas I-III
	Part A
	  Stanzas I-III
		The questions and statements of the stranger emphasizing the Knight's agony

	Part B Stanzas IV-IX	The visionary pursuit of beauty to the grot. Stanza IX is the transition and the beginning of a dream within the vision.
Response		
Stanzas IV-XII	Part C Stanzas X-XII	Away from the grot to the cold hill's side — a return to the mood and words of Part I — envelope pattern

Important to the thematic structure are the two geographical locations, the grot and the hill's side, both of which become symbols. The grot is associated with a past experience — a pleasant one shattered by a nightmarish dream. The hill's side is linked to the present — to the withered emotions of the Knight. Between the two places there is a cause-effect relationship.

Starting with these facts obtained through careful reading, one could begin to see the grot and the hill's side as symbols of two conditions of man in collision. On the one hand, the grot is related to the beautiful supernatural creature around whom are woven experiences appealing to the senses and related to the pursuit of beauty. This pursuit leads to the grot, wherein the pleasure of the vision is destroyed by the dream.

The dream relates to the real world of princes and warriors, to the cold hillside of life. By intruding upon the grot, the deathlike nature of the hill's side destroys the pursuit of beauty. A lack of faith in the supernatural or in ideal beauty rooted in sense experience leads to emotional death. The grot requires faith; the hill's side represents lost faith. Thus the symbolism offers a conflict between the Knight's visionary pursuit of beauty and the lack of faith of the real world. The effect of the collision is the spiritual despair of the Knight.

In addition to focusing the organization of his poem on the two symbols, Keats provides numerous other structural devices and links within each major section and between sections. In the stress upon key words and in the repetition of words and sentence patterns, moods and meaning are established.

In the first part (stanzas I-III), where the observer confronts the Knight, there is a beautiful pattern which creates a mood of barrenness and dying. The first two stanzas are exactly alike in structure—a question and details about the setting, expressed in images from nature. The questions stress what the observer sees in the Knight's situation and face: "Alone and palely loitering," and "So haggard, and so woe-begone." These descriptive words create a somber mood—an ominous introduction to the Knight's story. The details from nature which follow the question intensify the mood, for the emphasis is on the dying of nature and the absence of the birds. In addition, stress upon the harvest's being over and the squirrel's granary being full connotes the death associated with the approaching winter and intrudes an ironic note, since ultimately we learn that for the Knight the attempt to harvest his experience with the Lady has led to his own spiritual death. In this beautiful parallel structure we should note that lines 3 and 7 about the sedge and the squirrel parallel one another as do those about the birds and the harvest, thus creating an alternating rhythm of vegetation and animal images.

Stanza III intensifies the somber mood which suggests death or dying. Here Keats fuses images of nature with the Knight to indicate human suffering. The two flowers to which the observer compares the brow and cheek of the Knight are made emblems of anguish and dying. The use of the word *fading* to describe the rose and the repetition of the word *withered* (first used in line 3), as well as the reiteration through different words of the suffering visible in the Knight's face, all establish quite effectively the keynote of a mortal illness which is to dominate the poem.

The rest of the poem consists of the Knight's response to the unidentified observer. This response, the central dramatic incident, we have divided into two parts: stanzas IV-IX and stanzas X-XII.

At first the Knight's response seems to be a dramatic shift from the mood created in part A, for in stanzas IV-VII the emphasis is clearly upon the senses and upon the sensuous. The somber intensity of the musical quality of part A seems to relax and to take on the air of a supernatural exploration of the senses. Although many details connote that the woman is a supernatural creature, she is not a nightmare in the Knight's mind as he recalls the encounter with her. She is revealed as a vision, a dream, of beauty which he has been pursuing. Her beauty and her appeal to his senses are emphasized throughout this section. Sight, sound, taste, and touch are all vivid in the Knight's mind. Her hair, her foot, and especially her wild eyes—the details of sight. Her *sweet moan,* her song, her words of love in a strange language—sound. The *roots of relish sweet,* the *honey wild,* and the *manna dew* (note contrast with *fever dew* in line 10)—taste. The *kisses four*—the touch of soothing love.

It is not until the Knight and the Lady enter the elfin grot in stanza VIII that an ominous note reminiscent of part A intrudes—the weeping and sighing of the Lady. Here we have a foreshadowing that their comfortable retreat will be invaded when the dream within a dream occurs. The sensuous musical quality of this section is abruptly torn apart in line 34 by the painful cry, "Ah Woe betide!" The reference to the "cold hill's side" with emphasis on *cold* takes us back to the emptiness and dying of part A. Thus stanza IX serves as a transitional link in part B, looking back to the sensuous pursuit of beauty and leading up to part C, which emphasizes the horrible dream within a dream.

In the last part of the poem the words *pale* and *death pale* (line 38), although associated with kings, princes, and warriors, recall the description of the Knight in line 2 as *palely loitering,* and look forward to line 46 and intensify the mood of death in the real world. Stanzas X and XI depict by words and music the intrusion of the grim horrible world into the dream of the Knight. This interruption destroys not only the dream in the grot but also the vision or dream of pursuit of ideal beauty. The suspicion of this beauty is not directly uttered by the Knight but by the kings and warriors who represent the world outside of the vision. Their distrust of the beautiful woman leaves the Knight destroyed "on the cold hill's side"—a telling repetition of line 36.

It is not surprising, then, that in the last stanza the Knight himself corroborates the observations of the anonymous observer. The last three lines are thus an affirmative repetition of lines 2-5. The Knight is brought back to the real world where he has always been except for the dream vision which has failed.

The Knight's malady is the dying of his spirit, his disillusionment in the loss of the vision of beauty. He is left in the cold world bereft of the warm sensuousness of that vision. The real world apparently cannot sustain a faith in the vision of beauty, and without that faith the Knight, perhaps man, is left spiritually empty. The fatal contrast between the real world and the visionary world of beauty is, of course, presented through the two key symbols of the grot and the cold hill's side.

Structure of Fiction. Although the story in "La Belle Dame" has some bearing on the structure of the poem, the intricacy of the poetic devices is more important in the analysis above. In the structure of fiction some of these devices, such as symbols and patterns of imagery, are important. In fiction, however, the emphasis upon plot—the story or narrative which depicts a unified or purposeful sequence of events or which meaningfully relates events disconnected in time—forces the reader to observe the totality of a story or novel in different ways. These methods in turn can be applied to narrative poetry.

Plot structure is the basic organization of the events, details, or parts (scenes, chapters) of a story. In analyzing plot structure, the student is concerned with how and why the events are arranged as they are and whether the arrangement is effective. He will try to determine whether and how the plot is unified.

A study of the unity of structure is related to many aspects of literature. Point of view (see Glossary) defines the perspective from which a story is told and indicates whether and how the author has limited the unfolding of the plot. Concentration on a central character or on a major conflict can be important to unity. Even the consistency of an author's tone can unify diverse elements in a work. Sometimes the smooth flow of the chronology of events will be interrupted by the flashback, a deliberate movement to earlier events. This device is particularly effective in psychological fiction. At times an author will employ a subplot, another sequence of events which may or may not relate to the main plot or characters. Since a flashback or a subplot naturally interrupts the development of the central narrative, the key question involving unity is, "What is the relationship of the interruption to the structure?"

In some narratives, particularly those written before the twentieth century, one can analyze plot structure in terms of exposition, complication, climax, and denouement. In "The Ambitious Guest," Hawthorne uses these traditional ingredients. In the exposition of his story, the part which provides background for the reader, he establishes his two settings (the dangerous mountain environment and the cheerful and warm atmosphere inside the house), introduces the family and the guest, reveals essential information about the stranger, and prepares for the interplay between the guest and the members of the family. This interplay of the guest's vast ambition and the humble wishes of the family constitutes the complication or rising action—the movement of actions and conflicts from the beginning of the chief events to their climax. When the destructive slide descends, the climax, or high point of action toward which the complication has been moving, occurs with ironic and disastrous results. The denouement, or aftermath of the climax, allows Hawthorne to stress the irony and to state his theme. (For a fuller discussion of the story, see pp. 104-109.)

These traditional tools for analyzing the structure of plot will not be too useful for "Flowering Judas," a modern story. There is, for instance, no continuous part of the story which can be labeled exposition. Throughout the narrative the reader is given background material which helps him understand the two chief characters. The sequence of events does not move in a straight line, for Miss Porter dips back and forth between the one representative night of Braggioni's month-long courting of Laura and the pasts and futures of the two. In fact, the structure is based on the balancing of the author's account of that representative night and her commentary about her characters' pasts.

At the end of the story, the pattern culminates in two scenes which provide a climactic contrast: Braggioni's return to his wife and Laura's dream. Braggioni, who has callously rejected Eugenio, returns home and is treated like a savior by his wife. Laura, on the other hand, is tormented by a guilty conscience about Eugenio. Connected with this ironic reversal of the Judas role is the Judas tree, which, although referred to only briefly, becomes in Laura's dream a powerful symbol related to the ironic contrast at the end. The story has no denouement: closing as it does with Laura's dream, the plot becomes ambiguous in that the reader is left to contemplate the possibilities of Laura's fate. He is not told what it will be, whereas in "The Ambitious Guest" the fates of the people are quite clearly depicted.

In some narratives, unity of structure seems to be deliberately sacrificed; for example, a picaresque novel consists of a series of events in which the only common denominator is apparently a wandering hero or central character. However, even in a picaresque novel such as *Huckleberry Finn,* one can find a unity of meaning if he concentrates on the moral implications of all or most of the seemingly disconnected experiences of Huck and Jim.

At first glance the widely reprinted short story "Haircut" by Ring Lardner also seems to lack unity, chiefly because the narrator, a barber, is so garrulous that his conversation wanders aimlessly from person to person and incident to incident. One may be puzzled momentarily by the narrator's psychological process of association, whereby his mind almost consistently picks up a name or incident and moves to something associated with it. However, the reader, being more perceptive than the barber, eventually discovers that the death of a vicious practical joker named Jim Kendall was not an accident, as the barber believes, but a murder committed by a half-witted boy. Despite his rambling account the barber manages to give one all he needs to know to understand the situation: the harassment of the attractive Julie by Jim, the romance developing between Julie and young Doc Stair, the devotion of poor Paul to them, and the remark made by Doc which Paul took literally and which motivated his killing of Jim. As a result the reader is not surprised by the verdict of the coroner, Doc Stair, that Jim's death was accidental. Thus all of the plot pieces fall into place much more meaningfully than the barber himself knows, and the self-revelation of his stupidity and ignorance actually enhances the effect.

Although the psychological pattern affecting the barber's telling of the story is not very complicated, in some narratives the author will attempt to capture a more complex psychological makeup of people (for example, Joyce in *Ulysses* or Faulkner in *The Sound and the Fury*). In these seemingly chaotic works one must link his analysis of plot to understanding of the psychology of people. The disjointed account of actions, feelings, and thoughts may have a valid psychological unity.

In addition to the unity of structure in plot, one may also examine the completeness of the sequence of action. A plot can carry the development of a person's life from birth to death or between clearly defined points that finally fix the destiny of the central character. On the other hand, a plot may be segmental, dealing with a small portion of experience and leaving the results inconclusive or ambiguous.

Among the stories reprinted in this volume, both types of plots are represented. "The Ambitious Guest" provides the most complete and definite evolvement of plot. Despite the uncertainties created by the point of view in "Birthday Party" (p. 30), the plight of the wife seems clear: her basic incompatibility with her husband, as observed in the incident in the story, will continue. In "Old Mr. Marblehall" (reprinted on pp. 179-185), it is evident in the conclusion that the old man will not shock the town; the indifference toward him will exist until and after his death. On the other hand, "Flowering Judas" is designedly ambiguous and segmental. The reader knows that Braggioni's pursuit of Laura has only temporarily halted, but he cannot know whether Braggioni's persistence will ultimately destroy her. One is also aware of the pain involved in Laura's guilty conscience, yet he cannot determine whether, in her already confused state, she will be able to survive the emotional shock of this latest blow. Such uncertainty fits the lifelong unsettled existence of Laura.

OTHER PRINCIPLES OF ANALYSIS

Technique and Analysis. Other principles that a student should be aware of before he attempts to write a literary interpretation are closely related to what has already been discussed in this chapter. Throughout the analyses of examples, the techniques of authors have been emphasized — for instance, Shakespeare's command of metaphors and Keats' and Porter's sense of structure. The student of literature must recognize how a writer presents his emotions or ideas. The word *how* means the author's technique, the numerous methods he may use to shape his material. Awareness and analysis of technique will definitely lead one away from the literal approaches and may result in rich explorations of form and content.

The word *form* means the shape any literary work assumes as a result of *all* the technical resources employed by an author. *Content* is the material — ideas, emotions, events, people — which the author is shaping. A fusion of form and content occurs when the author has chosen and successfully employed the most suitable technical devices to develop his subject matter. Since it is often easier to talk about an author's ideas, the emphasis in literary analysis is too frequently placed upon content.

The importance of technique as it contributes to form has perhaps been best expressed by Mark Schorer in his essay "Technique as Discovery":

> Modern criticism has shown us that to speak of content as such is not to speak of art at all, but of experience; and that it is only when we speak of the *achieved* content, the form, the work of art as a work of art, that we speak as critics. The difference between content, or experience, and achieved content, or art, is technique.[2]

According to Schorer, "technique is the only means [an author]

2. Mark Schorer, "Technique as Discovery," *Hudson Review,* I (Spring 1948), 67.

has of discovering, exploring, developing his subject, of conveying its meaning, and, finally, of evaluating it."[3]

A knowledge of the various techniques available to an author involves an understanding of terminology. Terms and labels in themselves are not too useful; but, combined with a comprehension of what they stand for, they can become extremely valuable. To help students master terminology and recognize the importance of technique, this textbook provides, in addition to the present chapter, a glossary of terms and suggestions for analyzing fiction and poetry. All these discussions and tools are designed to lead the student into more complex analyses of literary works than he may previously have been accustomed to.

Multiple Interpretation. One should realize, however, that literary analysis can become extremely sophisticated and indeed controversial. A student of literature may be confused by what he encounters in the classroom and in the library. If he relies heavily on his teacher for interpretation, he may clutch at the teacher's ideas for the final analysis of a work. Yet he may find in the library or in a different classroom that other people think that they have *the* interpretation. He will notice that for some works there is an endless stream of varying interpretations. He will ask, "Who is right? What did the author really intend?"

To be truthful, these questions cannot be accurately answered because many literary works are so expansive and suggestive that they are subject to many interpretations. Even the seemingly clear and simple narrative poem "La Belle Dame" can be interpreted in at least two different ways. In this chapter the interpretation stresses the disillusionment of the Knight because the skeptical world has shattered his visionary pursuit of beauty. This is contrary to the conventional interpretation, which emphasizes the woman as an enchantress subtly seducing and destroying the Knight. In short, according to this latter view, the skepticism of the real world is valid.

"The Heavy Bear" can also be variously interpreted, especially if outside knowledge or research is applied. One can argue that it is a poetic rendition of a Platonic idea — the struggle within the soul between the irrational elements and reason. In this interpretation the bear becomes the symbol of the irrational. One could also urge that the poem portrays a conflict in Freudian

---

3. Ibid.

terms—the struggle between the *superego* and the *id*. Within this interpretation the bear is equated with the *id*, the powerful animal urges within man, which the *superego*, a restraining force, has to contend with. In Chapter 7, two different interpretations of "Flowering Judas" will be referred to as still another example of multiple interpretation.

Facing these opposite interpretations, can one dogmatically reject either of them? Perhaps John Ciardi, a poet and critic, has answered this question by saying, "The fact that a good poem will never wholly submit to explanation is not its deficiency but its very life."[4] The elusiveness of any literary text can be one of its chief virtues. Take away the connotative force of literature, and we no longer have literature. Therefore, it is unwise for one to allow the questions that arise amid confusion to drive him back to literal approaches or to utter timidity in analytical reading.

A student of literature needs to accept the validity of multiple interpretation. He should not be surprised that many interpretations of works like *Hamlet* and *Moby Dick* exist and that more are possible. He should, however, guard against the excesses of dogmatism and unrealistic in-reading (the imposing upon the literary work of the interpreter's own emotions or learning which may not be related to the story or poem). Instead of being quarrelsome and dogmatic, the student approaching "La Belle Dame," *Hamlet,* or *Moby Dick* should simply take his stand by supporting his position with evidence from the text as fully, logically, and effectively as possible. Discussions involving disagreements about interpretations need not be wasteful; in fact, they may stir up new insights.

The Affective Fallacy. To avoid the excesses of dogmatism and inappropriate in-reading, the student must exercise great control over his emotions and thinking processes. He must maintain sufficient detachment from a story or poem to analyze it logically. To do so is not easy, for anyone who is at all sensitive to imaginative literature knows that it frequently communicates the emotions of human experience so powerfully that it can have an overwhelming impact. Because the purpose of literature is to involve and engage readers, it may also appeal vividly to the imagination. However, one can write a reasonably objective analysis and still feel the emotional and aesthetic impact of the literary work. The analysis of "La Belle Dame" is organized,

4. John Ciardi, *How Does a Poem Mean?* (Boston, 1959), p. 779.

controlled, and thorough in providing evidence. Yet it makes vital the deep emotional experience of the Knight and at the same time provides ample evidence of an aesthetic appreciation of the skill of Keats in constructing the poem.

One could easily identify himself with the poem and allow it to lead him to subjective commentary. Such a response might go like this: " 'La Belle Dame' reminds us of the women we have known and of the sights which radiate beauty and the sounds which echo love. We savour the kisses, and with the Knight we enter the elfin grot. Thus are we drawn into a world of enchantment, a world reminiscent of the fairy tales we read in youth." Even worse would be a response in which a writer identifies his own emotional disturbances with the spiritual death of the Knight. At its worst such subjective identification could lead to an orgy of breast-beating.

This inability to separate the effects of a poem from the poem itself has been called the "affective fallacy" by W. K. Wimsatt, Jr., and Monroe C. Beardsley. Their definition of the term follows:

> The Affective Fallacy is a confusion between the poem and its *results* (what it *is* and what it *does*). . . . It begins by trying to derive the standard of criticism from the psychological effects of the poem and ends in impressionism and relativism.[5]

Beardsley and Wimsatt thus object to the kind of reading in which one interprets or criticizes the poem or literary work in terms of his own experience (relativism) or in which emotional and psychological responses of the reader (impressionism) substitute for objective analysis.

Although it is probably impossible to achieve in literary analysis the high degree of objectivity which Wimsatt and Beardsley seek, they nevertheless offer a useful point to the student of literature. Subjective involvement can blind a reader; it can lead to a blocking of the thought process. Of course, no one should deny the vigor of the appeal of literature: to do so would destroy the power of a play like *Macbeth*. However, in writing an interpretation of Macbeth's character, one would be unwise to denounce him heatedly because the reader hates murderers or believes in capital punishment.

Thus in his reading and in his writing of an interpretation,

5. W. K. Wimsatt, Jr., and M. C. Beardsley, "The Affective Fallacy," *Sewanee Review,* LVII (Winter 1949), 31.

one must try to separate his emotional responses from his intellectual analyses of technique and meaning. The student must place sufficient distance between his own emotions or prejudices and the literary text which he is examining. Good analytical interpretation will stem from a high degree of objectivity.

A SUMMARY OF PRINCIPLES

Because this chapter is intended as a primer to assist the student in analytical reading preparatory to writing interpretations, it may be wise to summarize the basic principles which have been stressed:

1) Although one may begin with a literal approach to a poem, story, or drama, he cannot rely solely on dictionary definitions of words, paraphrase, and summary.

2) One must distinguish between denotation, the literal approach to words, and connotation, the suggestive power of words or details.

3) One must also distinguish between a paraphrase or summary and an analysis of a literary work.

4) In order to analyze a work, one must always be aware of the context of the elements he is investigating. Analysis of context involves a logical process of relating details from which conclusions can be developed.

5) In order to analyze a poem or story, one must understand imagery so that it can lead him to a figurative reading of the work.

6) In the study of imagery the metaphor and the symbol are perhaps the most important tools of analysis.

7) One should look at a literary work not only in terms of its parts, but also in terms of the totality of structure to which these contribute.

8) One needs to comprehend techniques and the terminology involved in techniques before he can write a good interpretation.

9) The suggestiveness of the literary work creates opportunities for multiple interpretation, yet the student should avoid the excesses of dogmatism and unjustified in-reading. Any interpretation which he submits must be validated by the citation and interpretation of adequate evidence from the text.

10) To avoid committing the affective fallacy, one needs to maintain a high degree of objectivity and to stress evidence and logical procedures in his analyses.

Chapter 2

THE WRITING

OF A LITERARY INTERPRETATION

In addition to understanding the principles discussed in Chapter 1, the student should recognize the basic steps involved in writing an interpretation. In this chapter these steps will be discussed and illustrated.

During his preparation before writing his first draft of a literary interpretation, the student must pay close attention not only to his reading but also to the complicated procedure of shaping his insights. Too often he may concentrate so hard on the final version that he may forget that a long process of thought and note-taking is necessary before he has something sound or significant to say. Without intensive preparation, however, he will probably accomplish very little, and without careful note-taking he will impose an impossible burden upon his memory, especially if the literary selection being analyzed is lengthy and complex.

FIVE BASIC STEPS

At least five basic and sometimes indistinguishable steps are involved in the writing of an interpretation:

1) After careful and intensive study of the literary work and of preliminary notes, the student should settle upon a theme idea or a clear statement of his purpose. This will be the broadest generalization in the paper and should control all of the material.

2) The student should attempt to discover all of the passages (key words, actions, speeches, inner thoughts, comments of the author, etc.) which relate to his theme idea. Even before he has decided upon his purpose, he should have been taking notes, at least in his book. After he has a theme idea, or after he has narrowed down the assigned subject, he should go back over the

work, checking or revising his previous notes and adding new ones. For a story as brief as "Birthday Party" (p. 30), notes in the book would perhaps do; for a short paper, it is possible to compile a list of important passages and details on a sheet of paper, although this procedure can lead to confusion if one is not careful. However, for a longer work, especially a novel or a play, or even a lengthy story or poem, one would be wise to place his notes on cards with page numbers from the text, as if he were doing a research paper. No matter what method of note-taking the student uses, he should make the notes meaningful and useful; they should contain specific details, generalizations, interpretative comments, and anything else which will guide him during the process of writing. Some students prefer to take an additional step after making notes—that is, to jot down details and ideas relevant to the theme idea without much attention to order or logical sequence. This procedure gives the student the opportunity to get on paper some points which may be forgotten if left until later. Thus during the writing, both his notes and his random thoughts can be used for constructing an outline.

3) At all times the student must be aware that the theme idea has to be shaped in an orderly way. He will have to break down the generalization or generalizations in his theme idea. These smaller divisions must be logically and effectively arranged; in reality, they are the Roman numerals in an outline.

4) After the main divisions are established, the student should go back over his notes and select representative ones which will develop and support each division of his theme idea. These details must also be carefully arranged so that the outline will be complete.

5) Since the final paper must be more than an outline, the student must expand and interpret the passages and details which he uses; he must also explain his smaller generalizations clearly. He should avoid a series of sweeping statements, but he should not merely create categories and, like a file clerk, sort details into each one. He must go a step beyond by asking himself how and why these details support the generalization they are supposed to develop. In this way he can expand his outline into a theme. During the writing of the theme, he must be fully aware of the mechanics of his own style.

A PRACTICAL DEMONSTRATION

To see these suggestions in action, read the brief story "Birthday Party" very carefully and then go through the step-by-step approach to writing an analysis of it. Although one does not have to follow this procedure exactly as it is presented here, the emphasis on close reading and on orderly method will prove helpful.

Birthday Party[1]

They were a couple in their late thirties, and they looked unmistakably married. They sat on the banquette opposite us in a little narrow restaurant, having dinner. The man had a round, self-satisfied face, with glasses on it; the woman was fadingly pretty, in a big hat. There was nothing conspicuous about them, nothing particularly noticeable, until the end of their meal, when it suddenly became obvious that this was an Occasion—in fact, the husband's birthday, and the wife had planned a little surprise for him.

It arrived, in the form of a small but glossy birthday cake, with one pink candle burning in the center. The headwaiter brought it in and placed it before the husband, and meanwhile the violin-and-piano orchestra played "Happy Birthday to You" and the wife beamed with shy pride over her little surprise, and such few people as there were in the restaurant tried to help out with a pattering of applause. It became clear at once that help was needed, because the husband was not pleased. Instead he was hotly embarrassed, and indignant at his wife for embarrassing him.

You looked at him and you saw this and you thought, "Oh, now, don't *be* like that!" But he was like that, and as soon as the little cake had been deposited on the table, and the orchestra had finished the birthday piece, and the general attention had shifted from the man and woman, I saw him say something to her under his breath—some punishing thing, quick and curt and unkind. I couldn't bear to look at the woman then, so I stared at my plate and waited for quite a long time. Not long enough, though. She was still crying when I finally glanced over there again. Crying quietly and heartbrokenly and hopelessly, all to herself, under the gay big brim of her best hat.

Katharine Brush

A summary of this story would be relatively easy. A student probably would write: "'Birthday Party' deals with a wife's disappointment and a husband's anger when she attempts to celebrate his birthday by a birthday cake and an orchestral serenade in a restaurant where they are dining." A summary could, of course, be a bit more detailed than this, but the one sentence tells in objective fashion what actually happened.

However, such a summary, no matter how complete, will not reveal any special insight and will not serve as a firm foundation for a truly interpretative paper. The student must poke beneath the surface of the story, must examine the suggestive power of key words, and must find the real human experience which underlies this seemingly simple story. Using materials referred to in Chapter 1, the Glossary, and Suggestions for Analyzing Fiction, and following the five basic steps presented on pages 28-30, let us now take "Birthday Party" as our source and move away from a summary toward a genuine analysis and interpretation.

1) Theme Idea: Let us first consider the point of view (see Glossary and Suggestions for Analyzing Fiction) from which the story is told, since this is often a significant clue to the intentions of the author. We notice that the story is narrated by an unidentified observer, who merely happens to be sitting in the restaurant where the incident occurs. Our first impression of his report is that it is unbiased or objective because obviously the couple involved is not known to the narrator. Since we do not really know even the sex of the observer, we cannot say that this factor conditions his response to the incident. Yet the germ of the story, and our theme idea, must lie in what the observer tells us, for we have no other source of information and no other perspective.

We may then ask ourselves how this neutral narrator describes the moment of observed experience. Throughout the incident the observer seems to sympathize with the wife, and at the crucial moment he senses that she needs help, or at least sympathy. This recognition bursts into a direct criticism of the husband (by the narrator) in the third paragraph: "You looked at him and you saw this and you thought, 'Oh, now, don't *be* like that!' But he was like that. . . ."

Since the observer's attitude is so definite, Katharine Brush apparently intended it to be the main point of the story. Thus, through a study of the point of view, we can now move to a larger deduction. Our logical procedure leads us to the following theme idea: This incident of quick and cutting conflict represents a basic incompatibility between two people of entirely opposite natures—one strong and the other weak, one arrogant and the other meekly trying to please.

2) Notes: It is important that we record in notes the key words and phrases which led us to this conclusion about the theme of the story, for we shall use these specific details as evidence in our interpretative theme. Here are examples of notes we might record:

Note 1 — Narrator's reactions before the event

Husband: "self-satisfied face" — At minimal connotation, this phrase could simply mean complacency. At the same time, it could connote smugness, egotism, possibly arrogance.
Wife: "fadingly pretty, in a big hat" — This suggests fragility, as contrasted to her husband's smugness. The hat mentioned here must be linked with the last sentence; see next note. Also observe that before the man explodes in anger, she is described as beaming with "shy pride," again connoting fragility and also sentimentality.

Note 2 — Narrator's account of the reactions of the two to the incident

Husband: "hotly embarrassed, and indignant at his wife for embarrassing him." Utters a "punishing," "curt and unkind" remark to her. These reactions seem to bear out the implication of egotism and arrogance in the observation of his "self-satisfied" face. Even if he were shy, should he have cut her down for trying to please him?
Wife: The last sentence underscores her fragility and also connotes incompatibility in the word "hopelessly." The hat becomes important and plays up the basic irony, the backfiring of her little surprise. We get an image of two opposites: the woman broken emotionally and "the gay big brim of her best hat." She is not big but beaten; she is not gay; obviously the word "best" may be applicable to her hat, but not to her life.

Other notes could be presented, but these should give some idea of the function of notes in recording details and interpretations — that is, useful comments (even roughly phrased) which might be of value in the final paper.

3) Dividing the theme idea into smaller generalizations: By compiling and studying the passages relevant to our theme idea, we can derive some generalizations which will support it, and we are ready for a skeletal outline:

I. General statement of the conflict and tension
II. First impressions of the observer
III. Reactions of observer to the central conflict: the responses of the man and woman to her little surprise
IV. Emphasis on basic incompatibility

4) If we go back to our notes, we can see that they supply material for sections II and III of our outline. Actually I and IV are the introduction and conclusion and do not necessarily need material from our notes. Using our notes, we can now expand our outline so that it will be more meaningful to us when we write our paper. It will now look something like this:

I. General statement of the conflict and tension
II. First impressions of the observer indicating a difference in character between the man and woman
  A. Husband — "self-satisfied"
    1. Implies egotism
    2. May imply arrogance
  B. Wife
    1. "Fadingly pretty" connoting fragility
    2. "Shy pride" and sentimentality in having her husband's birthday celebrated somewhat publicly
III. First impressions of observer borne out by the reactions of the husband to the central incident and by the emotional defeat of the wife
  A. Husband
    1. Anger — hotly embarrassed and indignant
    2. Cutting, unkind remark
  B. Irony of the wife's plight: crying "under the gay big brim of her best hat"
IV. Emphasis on basic incompatibility

5) In writing the paper, we should closely correlate notes and outline. Since the introduction and conclusion are not fully covered in these sources, we must prepare them carefully so that our purpose and our ultimate conclusion will be clear to any reader. In the body of the paper we will put into sentences and paragraphs the ideas and details indicated in the outline and notes. In so doing, we will be careful to elaborate upon the basic interpretation wherever possible. Eventually, perhaps after sev-

eral attempts to harvest all of the careful preparations, we can offer the following essay:

An Interpretation of "Birthday Party"

In "Birthday Party," the private emotions of an inconspicuous couple burst momentarily into public view. From the point of view of the observer we learn the circumstances which ignite the emotional tension. But, more important, the narrator's observations prepare us for the conflicting responses of the husband and wife.

In fact, the narrator's first impressions of the couple are remarkably sound without his realizing their validity. The husband's face is classified as "self-satisfied" with the clear implication of an egotistical and possibly arrogant character behind it. The wife, on the other hand, is extremely feminine and both fragile and meek. She is "fadingly pretty," an indication that she is like a beautiful piece of fragile china somewhat marred by aging. In addition, when the cake is presented and the birthday song is played, the wife is pictured as beaming with "shy pride." These details clearly stress the subdued nature of her character. Obviously the occasion is a sentimental one for her, yet her emotions in responding to her prepared surprise are not excessive.

Her husband's reactions to her "little surprise" are excessive: he is "hotly embarrassed" and indignant at his wife for embarrassing him. In his reaction there is something cruel — something sadistic — for when he feels affronted by her public display of the occasion, he deliberately hurts her with a statement described as "some punishing thing, quick and curt and unkind." Thus the meek, shy fragility of the wife is crushed by the overwhelmingly powerful emotional response of the husband.

Only when she is terribly hurt by his actions and words, do her emotions pour forth in tears. Yet her tears are fully understandable: what she had intended as a sentimental tribute to her husband has turned into a bruising emotional nightmare. The reversal is painfully ironic and is graphically described in the last sentence: ". . . crying quietly and heartbrokenly and hopelessly, all to herself, under the gay big brim of her best hat." She is not big but beaten; she is not gay; the word "best" may be applicable to her hat, but not to her life.

That "gay big brim" is obviously a cover-up, a symbol perhaps of a hopeless attempt by the wife to conceal the basic incompatibility of two people whose characters and emotional make-up are vastly different. The story as presented through the observer is thus a conflict between her fragile meekness and his hard-heartedness, her sentimentality and his cold fury, her feeble attempt to please him and his sadistic desire to crush her. Behind this incompatibility there must be a long untold series of similar expressions of arrogance by the husband, who apparently knows that there is one person whom his ego can dominate and destroy — his wife. Even during his birthday party he defeats her.

The procedure demonstrated above does not solve all of the specific problems involved in the writing of an interpretative essay. Frequently a student will learn how to read a poem or story carefully and to take notes on it, yet he may be unable to shape his material and his insights into a sound and coherent essay. Further chapters, therefore, will emphasize the specific problems one is likely to encounter in writing an interpretation of a literary work.

Although many of the problems to be discussed are relevant to any form of expository writing, the emphasis will be consistently upon literary materials and the special difficulties caused by the need to correlate a literary text with a composition. The problems to be presented are derived from an examination of numerous literary interpretations written by students and professional critics. Illustrative material will be provided and discussed for almost every problem. For convenience we shall divide the problems into five general groupings: the theme idea as related to content and structure (Chapter 3); solidity of content (Chapter 4); organization (Chapter 5); selected matters of style (Chapter 6); and research in literary interpretation (Chapter 7).

Chapter 3

THEME IDEA

AS RELATED TO CONTENT AND STRUCTURE

One of the most crucial phases in writing an interpretation is limiting and defining one's purpose by means of a theme idea, which is usually the broadest generalization to be developed in an essay. Many papers have been ruined because students did not begin with adequate theme ideas. Any failure to develop a coherent and meaningful thesis will probably have profound effect upon both the content and organization of an essay. To avoid getting off to a disastrous start, the student must work hard on limiting and expressing his theme idea.

In limiting the subject matter of his essay, one must avoid the extremes of vastness and narrowness. Frequently a teacher will offer a broad subject simply to test whether a student can limit it — that is, can find his own central generalization suitable to the subject. A theme idea will be too vast and vague if the student merely puts into his own words the big subject the teacher has suggested. If the topic concerns some phase of Eudora Welty's style, for example, one cannot offer the following theme idea: "Miss Welty's style is effective." The special characteristic of the style to be discussed must be isolated and carefully delineated.

If one is asked to write an essay on the patterns of imagery in *Hamlet,* he has certain vital decisions to make in order to limit his subject satisfactorily and avoid the pitfall of trying to cover too much territory. Will he simply take the topic at face value and write in general about the imagery in the play? Or will he concentrate, for example, on the imagery related to decay in *Hamlet?* If he chooses the first path, he will have undertaken an impossible task; and, unless he can devote months and years to the subject (as Robert Heilman did for his book on the imagery in *King Lear*), he will have to resort to superficial coverage and sweeping generalizations. These, as we shall see in the chapter on solidity of content (Chapter 4), are two defects in literary analysis that must be avoided. On the other hand, the student who concentrates only on the images of decay has a better chance to achieve solidity of content. If, for example, he links these images to Hamlet's disillusionment, he will provide limitations for his theme idea and can avoid superficial coverage and vast generalities. Even so, he will have to limit his material further by carefully selecting the examples of imagery which can be placed fluently within his pattern of organization and which can yield the richest possible interpretations and fulfillment of the theme idea.

Sometimes, as a result of the human desire to simplify complex literary works, the student is driven to an opposite extreme: he will limit his theme idea so much that he can go nowhere. Although a rigorously limited thesis may be clearly defined, it may lose all complexity and all possibilities of advancing the subject beyond a routine cataloging of examples to prove a point that probably needs no proof. A student starting with the obvious theme idea that Huck Finn is lazy or that Hamlet is a murderer or that Polonius is pompous or that Prufrock is shy is not likely to say anything significant.

Even if a student can limit his topic to avoid the extremes of vastness and narrowness, he still has to express his theme idea as clearly and as fully as possible. A theme idea will be poorly expressed if a student chooses inexact words, garbles the syntax of the sentence stating his purpose, or attempts to impress readers with an elaborate display of language which buries the theme idea. (See Chapter 6, Matters of Style.) Although an introduction to an essay should be effective and attract the reader's attention, it is more important to inform him precisely of the purpose than to attempt to dazzle him with ornate words and phrases which circle the theme idea. The verbosity, like the inexact phrasing or poor syntax sometimes involved in the statement of theme ideas, will probably lead to a loss of focus on the thesis and poor development of the purpose.

A theme idea will be inadequately expressed if the student does not define the key terms he uses. For example, if he says that Miss Welty's style is classical, he must define the term *classical* or at least designate the ingredients of a classical style. If one is dealing with Hamlet as a tragic figure, he should establish the criteria or definition of the phrase *tragic figure* before he writes his essay. If he avoids this important problem of definition, he may not write on the subject with which he started, or he may simply make halting attempts to link Hamlet to specific elements involved in the definition of a tragic hero. If he can establish during the development of his theme idea the criteria of a tragic figure and can arrange them in a logical order, these can become the guidelines of the organization of his essay.

Everything said thus far indicates that the limitation and expression of a theme idea have vital relevance to the content which will evolve from it. If the theme idea is too big or too vague, the content is likely to consist of generalities. If the purpose is too limited, the content may be specific enough but insignificant and superficial. If the student cannot clearly express his theme idea or define his important terms, he may make it impossible to develop sound content.

The limitation and expression of a theme idea also have much bearing upon problems of organization. The theme idea is the source of control over the material to be used. This central purpose, if clearly defined, becomes the backbone of the essay, or, to change the figure of speech, the focus. Everything in the essay must be related to the theme idea. The entire process of writing a literary interpretation amounts to an orderly examination of parts stated or implied in the theme idea. If the thesis is carefully constructed, it may even provide the basic structure of the essay; that is, it can provide built-in patterns of organization which will guide one in the making of his outline.

EXAMPLES OF DEFINING THE THEME IDEA

In the following examples we are given three statements of theme ideas for three different essays. In each set of examples we move from a poor, vague theme idea to one that fixes the reader's attention precisely upon the generalization to be developed in the interpretation. Although a clear theme idea is no absolute guarantee of good organization or solid content, the chances are that the third statement in each case will yield the best essay. At least it will provide the clearest guideline for the student to exploit.

A paper analyzing Laura's character in "Flowering Judas"

1)   The purpose of this essay is to present a character study of Laura in "Flowering Judas." [Repeating the assigned topic,

this vague statement implies that everything about her character will be covered.]

2)   Laura, the chief character in "Flowering Judas," is a confused young woman. [Although Laura may be confused, this theme idea is indefinite because it does not specify or define clearly the nature of her confusion.]

3)   Although Laura, the chief character in "Flowering Judas," is portrayed as cold and indifferent to the people involved in the Mexican revolution, she is, ironically, alive with a painful consciousness of guilt. [This theme idea defines clearly enough a seeming contradiction in her character and at the same time provides a built-in, two-part organization for the essay: her coldness and her strong guilty conscience, especially in the climactic dream.]

A paper on the structure of "La Belle Dame sans Merci"

1)   In this paper I shall deal with the structure of "La Belle Dame sans Merci." [This theme idea merely restates the broad problem presented in the assigned topic and hence is inadequate.]

2)   In "La Belle Dame" there is a close relationship between the total structure and the poet's technique. [Although this theme idea links structure to technique, it does not limit or define that relationship.]

3)   In "La Belle Dame" an understanding of Keats' technical resources, such as his repetition of key words and phrases, his use of parallelism, and his handling of symbols, leads us to an appreciation of the intricate structure of the poem. [This statement defines the relationship between technique and structure and also provides guidelines for the organization of the interpretative essay.]

A paper on the basic emotions developed in "On First Looking into Chapman's Homer"

1)   A poet frequently creates moods and emotions. [This is an obvious generality that gets the student nowhere.]

2)   In the sonnet "On First Looking into Chapman's Homer," Keats stresses the emotional response to a discovery. [At least the poem and its central purpose are identified, but the specific emotion is still missing.]

3)   In the sonnet "On First Looking into Chapman's Homer," Keats effectively establishes the feeling of awe — the silent wonder — which affects the sensitive person during an experience

of momentous discovery. [The student now has a chance to subdivide and advance his theme idea.]

In these examples the emphasis has been upon a statement of the theme idea in one sentence. However, at times, especially when he is dealing with a complex story or a complicated emotional reaction, the student will need more than one sentence or even more than one paragraph to prepare for the development of his main purpose or theme idea. For example, a theme on the character of Laura might have the following longer statement of purpose:

> Into the characterization of Laura, the main character in "Flowering Judas," Katherine Anne Porter has infused much skillful irony. On the one hand, she portrays Laura as cold and restrained in her response to those around her. Yet in her relationship with Eugenio, Laura displays a powerful feeling of guilt which could not reside in one whose emotions have been dulled by disappointing experiences. This juxtaposition by Porter of the coldness that seems to dominate most of the story and the searing conscience that bursts forth at the end establishes a meaningful and effective irony in the characterization.

In this case a fuller statement of purpose develops and clarifies the theme idea so that any reader will be completely aware of the intent of the essay.

The necessity of defining key terms or the complexity of the subject matter can lead a student to use two or three paragraphs to present his theme idea. In such cases, the student must be careful not to allow the introduction to dominate the essay or to become the essay. In a paper of five paragraphs, a reader would not expect three of them to express the theme idea. If a theme idea is so complex that it requires several paragraphs of explanation, then the development of the ideas in the body of the essay would automatically require considerably more space.

PLACEMENT OF THEME IDEA

The exact placement of a theme idea sometimes disturbs students writing a literary interpretation. Preferably it should come in the first part of the essay, even in the first paragraph. This position will be helpful to both the author and his readers.

The author thus provides himself a master plan that can control the evolution of his paper. By encountering the theme idea early in the essay, the reader will know exactly what the purpose and limitations of the effort are. He will also discover definitions of important terms in the theme idea. If the thesis is so complex that it requires two or more paragraphs of development, then the student must make these the first section of his essay.

In this book there are two examples of theme ideas contained in one sentence and placed in the first paragraph: "Analysis of 'On First Looking into Chapman's Homer'" (pp. 56-58), and "'La Belle Dame' and 'The Heavy Bear'" (pp. 81-82). In each of the essays "The Old Man and the Town" (pp. 72-75) and "Pessimism, Optimism, or Paradox?" (pp. 99-101), the theme idea requires longer treatment; hence the entire first paragraph is devoted to it.

At times a theme idea can be saved for a climactic position; that is, the author of an interpretation may feel it necessary to build up to his main point rather than to reveal it immediately. This approach is difficult, for there must be tight control over everything in the essay so that the reader can be skillfully led to the ultimate purpose. It takes an experienced writer to handle this approach, to maintain discipline while the theme idea is being withheld. (For example, see the interpretation of "Birthday Party," p. 34.) Even more difficult is the kind of interpretation which never states its theme idea directly either at the beginning or in a climactic position. The idea can be implied, but everything must be related to the implied backbone of the essay. Since literary interpretation is really exposition and is not intended to be creative writing (the writing of poetry, fiction, or drama) or to inspire tricks of writing, the student would perhaps be wiser to place the theme idea early in his essay.

Chapter 4

SOLIDITY OF CONTENT

An essay can be well written and clearly organized, but still say little or nothing. In the writing of interpretative essays, the student will discover that nothing, including an outstanding style, can compensate for empty content. To avoid such emptiness, the student must, as we have seen, start with a significant and well-defined theme idea. The material relevant to this idea and the treatment of the material are crucial in literary analysis. If the content is to be sound, the subject matter must be complex enough and the development must be thorough. The details used to develop a theme idea will come from a careful reading of the text and, if necessary, from research.

Sound content will be possible only if the student allows the reading experience to stimulate his thinking. Originality of interpretation is a virtue in literary criticism, especially since literature does evoke multiple interpretations. Yet the original thinking has to be supported by careful presentation and analysis of details and ideas. Otherwise the originality will be like a rocket which is destroyed because it veers from its flight path.

Many of the problems that students have with the content of their themes are due to a failure to understand what details are or to a tendency to misuse them. What are details? They are anything in a text which can be quoted, summarized, or para- phrased. In a story they can range from actions and words to the author's own comments. In a play they can even be stage direc- tions. In a poem, details are key words, actions, or thoughts (those directly stated). If research is being applied to a literary work, then the details would be the factual information or quotations derived from a study of materials outside the literary text. For example, if one were writing a research paper on Keats' sonnet about Chapman's Homer, he might wish to discuss information about Keats' writing of the poem, about Keats' reading as related to the poem's content, or about other poems by Keats bearing on the investigation.

Much of this chapter will deal with the misuse of details; at the end, a procedure for incorporating them properly into interpretative essays will be recommended.

GENERALIZATIONS VERSUS ANALYSIS

The quickest way to misuse details is to ignore them. Frequently our past training or habits of thought cause us to generalize and to forget about the evidence for our conclusions. In writing literary interpretations we must deal with generalizations about the work. We may be able to draw excellent conclusions and relate them to a theme idea, but if we do not develop them by citing and analyzing the details upon which they are based, then we are asking our readers to accept our views without seeing the evidence. The burden of proof lies with the author of the essay, not with his readers. If the author is unable to support his generalizations, then he will encounter a major problem if he seriously desires to put substance into his papers.

Scattered Generalizations. The worst use of generalizations occurs when the student simply ranges sweepingly over and beyond a literary work with no controlling theme idea in his essay. An example from a paper on *Moby Dick* follows:

> *Moby Dick* is a vast study of whales and human beings. It is a mixture of expository, narrative, and dramatic writing. Death broods over the book, and fate is an important subject in it.
>
> The book covers man from the most ignorant to the most intellectual; from the most faithful to God to the most defiant of Him. The land and the sea are opposing symbols. It is Moby Dick, however, who dominates the symbolical structure of the novel.
>
> Some claim that both Ahab and Ishmael reflect Melville's feelings. If this is true, Melville must have been deeply disturbed about the perplexing ambiguities of man's existence.

In this series of unfocused and badly scattered generalizations, one will find material for many significant essays on the book: the brooding nature of death and fate and their relationship to atmosphere; the land and sea as symbols; Moby Dick as a symbol; the autobiographical implications of the novel; and so forth. Almost every generalization is in itself a theme idea, which would have to be limited. Yet each could be richly developed by citation and analysis of details from the book.

The Unadvanced Theme. A student's struggles with generalizations and his failures to understand the function of details in his writing are clearly demonstrated in the unadvanced theme, an essay which starts with some generalization (even a well-defined one) but never develops it. Space is filled by repetition of the same thought or thoughts in different words. As an example, examine the following theme on "Flowering Judas":

> In "Flowering Judas" Katherine Anne Porter uses irony to condemn Braggioni. The irony is conveyed by her choice of words and by means of contrasting details.
>
> Many of Miss Porter's descriptive words are sarcastic and make Braggioni the villain of the story. Even though he is supposed to be a reformer and revolutionist, he turns out to be evil.
>
> By contrasting the ideals surrounding Braggioni with his actual performance, Miss Porter establishes irony. By means of this and other contrasts, the reader is made aware of Braggioni's fraud. Thus Laura emerges as the heroine of the story.
>
> The author's use of irony becomes apparent if one carefully observes the sarcastic words used to describe Braggioni and the numerous contrasts in the story.

This theme advances very little. After establishing as his theme idea the two devices of irony in paragraph one, the writer deals with each in separate paragraphs. In paragraph two, the only new thought occurs in the dependent clause of the second sentence. In paragraph three, only the last sentence, a generalization, intrudes a new note. The last paragraph merely repeats what has already been vaguely said several times. The theme very badly needs reshaping: elimination of the excessive repetition of the theme idea and development of the two-part structure through details and interpretation.

Undeveloped Paragraphs. A definite sign that a student writing a literary analysis is having trouble developing generalizations is the incorrect use of paragraphs containing only one or two sentences — a defect also apparent in the unadvanced theme above. Such short, choppy paragraphing is sometimes due to a failure to link related thoughts and details into one solid unit. If the difficulty cannot be attributed to this factor, then the student is providing topic sentences which are small generalizations but is not developing them. When there are many of these undernourished topic sentences, the content of the theme becomes skeletal. The following example consists of the last four paragraphs of a theme about Biff in *Death of a Salesman*. The student has been building his theme to a high point; then the choppy paragraphing intrudes and ruins the content by introducing stillborn ideas:

> The focal point in Biff's character is self-recognition, which emerges in the dynamic conflict between him and his father.
>
> As part of his understanding of himself he has to perceive the falseness of his father's dream.
>
> The fraud in his own life, so fully influenced by his father, must also come dramatically into his consciousness. He has to realize, for example, that the inflated glory of his football days has not been transferred to the realistic arena of life.
>
> Thus the final irony of the play lies in the contrast between Biff's full self-recognition and Willy's clinging to his false dream to the very last action — his suicide, his sacrifice of himself so that Biff can be what he no longer cares to be.

Although the writer is aware of Biff's discovery of himself, it is treated rather skimpily in these short paragraphs; obviously details and more complex analysis are needed to give flesh to the skeleton.

Difficulty with generalizations will range from the incoherent conglomeration in the theme on *Moby Dick* (p. 43) to isolated instances in good essays. Even in a fairly solid paper a student may leave one generalization or even several undeveloped. Of course, if the idea is obvious, it needs no documentation; but if it is provocative or controversial, then it must have evidence to support it. It is the responsibility of the author of a literary work to pin down his big generalization — his theme idea

—and all significant, complex, or controversial ideas related to it.

When unsupported generalizations offer little or nothing to the reader, it is the author's responsibility to clarify the questions which arise. Since interpretations of a specific work can be diverse and at times highly debatable, the student has an even greater obligation to support his views. The same process of logic applicable to our opinions on controversial social and political issues should operate when we attempt to analyze literary works.

INEFFECTIVE MIXTURE
OF SUMMARY AND ANALYSIS

As we have already seen, pure summary avoids interpretation entirely and hence can never lead to solidity of content, even though ample details are present. Even when the student realizes that he must break from summary if he is to achieve worth-while content, he may encounter another problem: ineffective mixture of summary and interpretation. Summary can be such a strong crutch that even when one is aware of its superficiality, he cannot discard it entirely. This problem occurs when one does not have a clear conception of his purpose or a clear mastery of the pattern of organization of his essay. Without such purposeful planning, the plot details will emerge as dominant, and the interpretative comments, many of which are generalizations, will be buried.

Below, a summary of "Flowering Judas" has been carried a weak step forward by the addition of a few interpretative comments which are placed in brackets wherever possible.

"Flowering Judas" deals with [a representative experience of] Laura, a young American involved in the Mexican Revolution. She is courted each night by Braggioni, the leader of the revolutionary movement. He patiently pushes his attentions upon her, and she resists. [There is irony in the combination of his unattractive physical bulk and ardent nature when compared to her physical attractiveness and restraint.]

During the description of the courting we learn something about the past and present activities of both Laura and Braggioni. Both have lost their idealism in regard to the revolution. Yet Braggioni's followers consider him an ideal revolutionist, a savior. [This feeling adds another irony to the story.] Laura's loss of faith is the latest in a series of disappointments in her life. [Hence she is left completely disturbed and confused.]

During the courtship Laura refers to Eugenio, a revolutionist who is dying because of an overdose of tablets which Laura had brought him in prison. In rejecting Eugenio as a fool, [Braggioni demonstrates his basic inhumanity].

Unable to win Laura, Braggioni temporarily returns to his long-suffering wife and has a reconciliation with her. [In this incident lies another irony: as she washes her husband's feet an image of Christ is created, yet the reader senses that his persistent infidelity to her will continue.]

Meanwhile, Laura dreams that Eugenio calls her a murderer and offers her bleeding flowers from the Judas tree outside her window. She awakens and is unable to go back to sleep.

Although we can detect some interpretative comments, they seem lost in the heavy framework of plot summary. In addition, they seem to have no purpose, no theme idea, and no direction other than that imposed by the story. (See the discussion of running commentary in the section on organization in Chapter 5.) Because these comments represent feeble attempts to intrude some interpretation into a summary, the content of the essay lacks solidity. Yet if one examines these comments carefully, he can see that the author threw away an opportunity to focus his theme on irony and to subordinate plot details to his analysis of that technique.

The domination of plot details can occur even when the student has a theme idea and a pattern of organization. Often a student will make his transition from paragraph to paragraph by introducing the new unit with a plot detail. If this practice is frequent or if the plot details progress beyond the first sentence of the paragraph, then the student creates a framework of plot summary and gives the impression of summarizing when he may actually be offering some worth-while development of his insights. The way to avoid this difficulty is to focus on an idea relevant to the theme purpose as one moves from paragraph to paragraph. In this connection we should note the difference between the following two introductory sentences about the Knight's spiritual despair in "La Belle Dame":

1) The Lady takes the Knight to the grot and there begins to cry.

2)   When the Lady takes the Knight to the grot and begins to cry, we get the first premonition in the Knight's narrative that his experience of pursuing beauty through the senses will be shattered.

The first sentence, a pure plot detail, may very well lead to further summary. In the second version the plot detail is subordinated and the interpretative comment is given the prominent position in the main clause. The author of the paragraph is now ready to connect the premonition to the dream, where the actual destruction of the vision occurs.

In practice, details from the literary work should be subordinated to the framework and interpretation of the student's paper. Details are used as evidence, as material to be analyzed. If used in any other way, they will dominate and in effect become plot summary.

THE SCISSORS AND PASTE APPROACH

As we have indicated, quotations from the literary work or from outside sources can be considered details. To some students (and even to some professional scholars and critics), quotations become the main content of the essay. The procedure they use is to establish a central purpose, to clip and arrange a series of quotations related to that idea, and to provide a few words of commentary — the glue — between the quotations. At times the glue is omitted, and the quotations are put down back to back. This process should be called the scissors and paste approach to literary analysis. It is obviously a fallacious approach for several reasons. It amounts to little more than a process of labeling and cataloging quoted details — a file clerk's or mail sorter's job. It provides no rich synthesis of the materials used. Most important, it throws the real burden of interpretation on the reader of the essay, who is asked to examine the quotations himself, without any real assistance from the author. If the quotations selected are worth-while, they would probably be full of implications and suggestions which could lead to important interpretations. If a quotation is not significant, then it probably should be put in the words of the author of the essay or omitted. Sometimes the quoted detail can be cut and integrated into a sentence in the paper. (See the discussion of the integration of quotations in Chapter 6.)

Actually it is wise to limit the number of long quotations. Those used, however, should be extremely important to the inter-

pretation being developed. If they are important, they will un-
questionably need careful analysis and not a thin spreading of
glue.

The following is an excerpt from a student's theme on fate in
Oedipus the King:

> All of the characters of the story believe in the fates and
> in prophecy, but a belief in God is also expressed. Three
> distinct beliefs are illustrated: that destiny is controlled by
> the fates, that individual lot is predestined by God, and that
> Fate is determined by man himself.
>
> Illustrations of the first belief are found in these quota-
> tions: "Oh Healer [the god, Apollo], will you send doom like a
> cloud or weave it like nightfall of the past?". . . "It is not from
> me your fate will come; that lies within Apollo's competence,
> as it is his concern.". . . "Death will not come to me through
> sickness, or in any natural way. I have been preserved for
> some unthinkable fate."
>
> Jocasta shows her faith in God's plan when she asserts,
> "It is God himself who can show us what he wills, in his own
> way." And Oedipus cries out in despair, "If I were created so,
> born to this fate, who could deny the savagery of God?" Creon
> also states, "God's will has not been wholly revealed to
> me. . . . We had best discover clearly what is to be done."
>
> The third tenet is also proved by many statements:
> "Apollo brought my sick, sick fate upon me, but the blinding
> hand was my own.". . . "Evil not done unconsciously, but
> willed . . . the greatest griefs are those we cause ourselves."
> . . . "When you were here, you served your own destruction."
> . . . "You are serving your own doom."

After establishing three categories for filing in the first paragraph, the student offers no more than a series of quotations to
illustrate each one. A few words of the author introduce each list
of quotations, but most of the quoted lines do not even have glue
between them. The reader is abandoned to wander through a per-
plexing maze. At least he will see an example of the scissors and
paste approach at its worst.

MISREADING OF DETAILS

Still another way of mishandling details and of destroying
solidity of content occurs when the student misreads the work he

is attempting to analyze. As was stressed in Chapter 1, there is a close correlation between how carefully one reads and how successful his essay is. If a detail is blatantly misread or misconstrued and the misreading becomes a part of an interpretation, then the student jeopardizes a part or all of his essay. Any generalization based on a misreading of details would almost automatically be invalid. In addition, if one provides too few details to support the big sweep of a generalization, he will distort the inductive reasoning process and possibly be accused of misreading. Another kind of mishandling of details occurs in extreme cases of academic in-reading when a critic imposes upon a literary work tons of irrelevant details from material outside the work—for example, from myths. Here, however, we shall be concerned with two bothersome kinds of misreading: unconscious slanting and a reduction of figurative meaning to literal equations.

Unconscious Slanting. Although details and quotations are extremely vital to interpretation, even the most capable interpreter can mar the content of his essay by unconsciously slanting them. One might become so convinced that his interpretation is right that he may distort the details he uses, take them out of context, or omit some which might change the interpretation or contradict the main point. If a theme idea has not been carefully developed, one can unconsciously force details to fit the purpose rather than derive the purpose from the details he has discovered in his reading.

As an example of unconscious slanting caused by omission of details, we can refer to an essay that might be written on the character of Laura. If one goes through the major part of "Flowering Judas," he can find ample evidence to support the interpretation that Laura is cold, that she denies any fulfillment of her emotions. To maintain such an interpretation, one would have to omit the climactic scene of the book, the powerfully symbolic dream which takes us deeply into Laura's mind and emotions. By omitting consideration of this sequence, one could slant the evidence to establish a thesis that Laura is emotionally dead, but the result would be false, for the dream shows that she is vividly alive with guilt feelings.

Whereas the essay above would be illogical because vital details or important context is omitted, the following paragraph from a paper on Oedipus is slanted because one detail is taken out of the total context of the play:

To determine Oedipus' attitude toward the gods, we must examine his statements about the oracles. As the oracles were the gods' means of communicating with men, one must have confidence in the validity of the oracles to have confidence in the gods. It is evident by the middle of the play that Oedipus no longer has respect for the oracles, for he rashly states: "So! Why then, Jocasta, should we study Apollo's oracle, or gaze at the birds screaming over our heads—these prophets who announced that I would kill my father? He's dead, buried, below ground. And here I am in Thebes—I did not put hand to sword." Oedipus, then, is a man who, instead of turning to the gods for strength and assistance with his trouble, scorns them and their sacred oracles, placing faith only in himself.

In this paragraph the student is taking a single speech and representing it as Oedipus' consistent attitude toward the oracles. By taking one passage out of context, he ignores several facts. Not long after the speech cited, Oedipus discovers that the dead man is not his father and that the prophecy has not been contradicted. As a result he immediately resumes his search for the murderer (as the oracle has dictated) and for his own identity. In addition, the fact that Oedipus is constantly running from his fate, only to face it, shows how much he basically fears and respects the oracles. The one quotation out of context cannot support the point the student is making, although he makes it with perfectly sincere intentions.

Literal Equations. If in a theme one demonstrates that he is taking details out of context and accepting them at face value, he is probably approaching his reading and writing too literally. For example, in paragraph twenty-five of "Flowering Judas" one can find some phrases describing Braggioni which, if accepted uncritically, put him in a favorable light. Miss Porter says, "Not for nothing has Braggioni taken pains to be a good revolutionist and a professional lover of humanity." One can leap to the phrases "a good revolutionist" and "lover of humanity" and present evidence for a very positive analysis of Braggioni's character. Yet the beginning of the sentence, "Not for nothing," and the word "professional" placed in front of "lover of humanity" qualify his magnanimity sarcastically, as do the rest of the immediate context and the persistent play of ironic commentary upon him throughout the story. Yet the literal acceptance of the flattering phrases could make an essay based upon them and upon other similar evidence totally invalid.

Equally disastrous is the display in students' essays of a literal-minded equating of figurative elements in a literary work with exact counterparts of meaning. In themes students have responded in precisely this way to the imagery of Shakespeare's Sonnet 73:

> That time of year thou mayst in me behold
> When yellow leaves, or none, or few, do hang
> Upon those boughs which shake against the cold,
> Bare ruin'd choirs, where late the sweet birds sang.
> In me thou see'st the twilight of such day
> As after sunset fadeth in the west,
> Which by and by black night doth take away,
> Death's second self, that seals up all in rest.
> In me thou see'st the glowing of such fire
> That on the ashes of his youth doth lie,
> As the death-bed whereon it must expire
> Consumed with that which it was nourish'd by.
>   This thou perceivest, which makes thy love more strong,
>   To love that well which thou must leave ere long.

In an attempt to present figurative reading, students have literally mangled the first quatrain. The yellow leaves falling become the loss of hair in old age (ultimately baldness), and the shaking boughs equal the infirm limbs of an old man. It is true that the three different images — the death of winter, the "black night," and the expiring fire — are related to the human problems of aging and dying. But it is unnecessary to seek exact equations between these and the dying beloved one who, as the spokesman in the poem, has created these images. Such oversimplification not only makes the poetic images ludicrous but also defeats the opportunity to achieve solidity of content in an essay on a complex and variously interpreted poem.

THE SUPERFICIAL ANALYSIS

An extremely bothersome kind of interpretative essay is the superficial analysis, which, although not entirely a failure, definitely lacks solidity of content. Such a paper may be based on a theme idea seemingly adhered to and developed; it also may be adequately organized and correctly written. Yet the interpretation offered is insignificant because the original idea is too limited (see the earlier discussion of theme idea in Chapter 3), or because the student has used only obvious details and derived weak interpretations from them, even though he may have begun with a complex theme idea. Superficiality occurs because one takes the easy path. A writer avoiding complex problems involved in his subject will rarely create solid content.

What is considered superficial depends, of course, on the judgment of an instructor. But because the student does not always understand the comment *superficial* when it appears on a theme, we need to examine the problem fully. For example, it would be easy to supply details that Ahab in *Moby Dick* is a monomaniac and to offer a few obvious comments. A workman-like but superficial theme could result. It is much more difficult to treat Ahab's monomania as a psychological phenomenon involving causes and effects. The student writing the superficial theme would attribute the cause to the important event in Ahab's life, the loss of his leg. But the perceptive student will start with that event and see it as the beginning of a complex inner brooding. He will note that the loss of the leg, the original cataclysm, becomes so dominant in Ahab's mind and emotional reactions that the whale is to the captain the symbol of all evil, universal evil. Some critics have even associated the ferocious monomaniacal drive of Ahab with the myth of Prometheus or with the concepts of Freud, especially in regard to the frustrating effect the loss of his leg has upon Ahab.

The difference between the superficial and perceptive presentation of content can be observed in another example involving Ahab. The student willing to start with a fairly obvious point and to develop it will never get beyond dealing with Ahab's traits. He could fill up several pages listing the various manifestations of a churning restlessness in Ahab, but the theme would probably consist of a long series of details, most of which would be self-explanatory, and a few interpretative generalizations. On the other hand, the student trying to cope with complexity would be willing to face a larger issue — a controversial issue: Is Ahab a tragic figure? The person taking this approach would subordinate Ahab's restlessness and the agony connected with it to the basic question he is trying to answer. He would, for example, attempt to determine whether Ahab commits hubris (defined by the Greeks as pride whereby man elevates himself to godhead) and whether he tries to defy fate, particularly as seen in the implications of Fedallah's prophecies. Although this topic might become unmanageable, it could be limited and still be rewarding, especially if it deals with the paradox of evil coming from Ahab's attempt to destroy evil.

To visualize the superficial paper, read the following discussion of the theme of reconciliation in *The Tempest:*

> *The Tempest* seems to put the theme of general reconciliation to its greatest possible use. In the conclusion, all old enmities are forgotten and all wrongs pardoned in a simple and straightforward manner.
>
> As in *The Winter's Tale,* Shakespeare deals in *The Tempest* with the reunions of long-separated friends and families, the reconciliation of enemies, and the complete forgiveness of wrongs. Prospero is reunited with his usurping brother Antonio, and they are naturally reconciled. Even Caliban, in spite of his wicked plots, is forgiven and left alone on the island in a state of simple happiness. Prospero, at last given a chance for revenge against his wrongdoers, does not take hold of his opportunity, but lets his wisdom rule his actions and grants complete forgiveness to his enemies. He, in fact, unites the two feuding kingdoms through the marriage of their two heirs.
>
> Everyone is left to his own devices, getting off with merely a lecture from Prospero. There is a general reconciliation and forgiveness, leaving a group of close and happy friends on the island, once characterized by strife and disunity.

In paragraph one this essay offers as a theme idea a topic which many students of the play have commented upon — general reconciliation. In paragraphs two and three we are given details to support the purpose. Yet it is clear that the essay is superficial because the concept of reconciliation has been oversimplified and because the student has chosen the most obvious details he could locate. Any perceptive reader would notice, for example, that very little is done with Prospero's reconciliation to social existence by his renunciation of supernatural power. Another way to approach the subject would be to relate the theme of reconciliation to natural and moral order, or hierarchy, as seen in those who people the island. This sense of hierarchy is a form of reconciliation of man's place, primarily in moral gradations. Still another possibility would be to discuss the poetic imagery and its relationship to the theme of reconciliation.

The student of literature must constantly strive to go beyond routine, oversimplified development of theme ideas. If he is to remain in the spirit of the literature he is interpreting, he must be bold and even speculative. He must be willing to cope with complex problems. If he is unwilling, then he is not likely to meet the requirements of solidity of content which are discussed in this chapter.

THE THREE-STEP PROCEDURE:
A PATH TO SOLID CONTENT

In dealing with a lack of solidity of content, we have thus far emphasized faulty handling of details in overuse of generalizations, in excessive plot summary, in the scissors and paste approach, in the misreading of details, and in the superficial theme. The way to avoid most of these problems is to conceive of analytical interpretation as a process which involves three steps operating simultaneously: (1) generalizations; (2) details related to them; and (3) analysis and interpretation of the details in terms of the generalizations they support. This procedure applies to the theme idea and its major divisions and to many of the individual paragraphs in an essay.

The operation of the three steps together is crucial. Without the buildup to the third one, the student is not likely to write sound analysis. Step one, which involves a meaningful controlling generalization and topic sentences of paragraphs, cannot by itself constitute an essay. If within a paper one were to have little more than a series of topic sentences, the content would be undernourished. The following sentence offered as the content of a paragraph on Keats' sonnet "On First Looking into Chapman's Homer" (reprinted on p. 56) would fulfill step one but would be inadequate: "That the discovery depicted in Keats' sonnet enlarges man's outlook can be seen in the three kinds of explorers in the poem."

The student can improve this undernourished paragraph by adding a list of details to support the topic sentence (step two):

> That the discovery depicted in Keats' sonnet enlarges man's outlook can be seen in the three kinds of explorers in the poem. Keats has encompassed man's culture. The stargazer has swept his eyes over the firmament. And Cortez has gazed upon the vast Pacific.

Although this paragraph is better than the scissors and paste approach, which also combines steps one and two, it does little more than provide three examples supporting the topic sentence.

Complex interpretation, or the fulfillment of step three, frequently demands more than the statement of a generalization — the label — and a list of details such as those in the paragraph above. At the same time, step three must grow out of the relationships between generalizations and details. Since, as we have noted, literature is highly suggestive and connotative, the student cannot rely solely upon a direct unfolding of details. He will have to be led by them to perceptive interpretation. He must ask himself: "What do the details imply? How are they really related to the point they are supposed to support?" These questions take the student to step three.

The sonnet below is followed by an analysis and then an evaluation of the analysis in terms of the three-step procedure. Note how the first paragraph of the analysis tries to answer the above questions and to employ the three steps together. The paragraph thus carries forward the beginnings of analysis in the examples under step one and step two.

On First Looking into Chapman's Homer

Much have I travelled in the realms of gold,
And many goodly states and kingdoms seen;
Round many western islands have I been
Which bards in fealty to Apollo hold.
Oft of one wide expanse had I been told
That deep-browed Homer ruled as his demesne:
Yet never did I breathe its pure serene
Till I heard Chapman speak out loud and bold.
Then felt I like some watcher of the skies
When a new planet swims into his ken;
Or like stout Cortez when with eagle eyes
He stared at the Pacific — and all his men
Looked at each other with a wild surmise —
Silent, upon a peak in Darien.

John Keats

Analysis of "On First Looking into Chapman's Homer"

A. Keats' sonnet on Chapman's Homer communicates magnificently the sense of awe that comes with any discovery which enlarges man's outlook. That the discovery is significant can be seen in the vastness of territories covered by the three kinds of explorers in the poem. Keats, the explorer of culture, has traveled widely in the golden realms of man's cultural heritage. The stargazer, the explorer of the heavens, has scanned the endless expanse of the firmament. Cortez (really Balboa), the explorer of earth, and his men have gazed out over the enormous stretch of water known as the Pacific. The momentous discoveries each explorer makes involve the physical universe (heaven and earth) and the intellectual kingdom. The sense of movement in the image of the cultural traveler and in the eyes of the star-gazer and of Cortez add to the pinpointing of the chief discovery — Chapman's translation of Homer — in the midst of the vastness.

B.   It is the response to the discovery which each makes that provides the rich emotional and intellectual impact of wonder or awe. The experience is communicated by Keats through a contrast between the vigor involved as the object of discovery makes its impact and the accompanying response of silence. The object of discovery in each case looms large through the senses. Chapman is pictured as speaking out *loud and bold;* the planet *swims* suddenly into the vision of the gazer (the pinpointing of a sight object in a vast background); and the enormous Pacific dazzles the *eagle eyes* of Cortez. In contrast to the vigor of the experience — the impact of the object discovered — the response is gentle. Keats' response to Chapman comes through a quiet sense image of breathing serene air. The power in Chapman's clarion ring also contrasts noticeably with the complete outward silence of Cortez and his men. In both instances the observer and participator is struck speechless with awe. In Cortez' case the only sense activity is the gazing of the men at each other. This activity of the men's eyes amid the silence captures effectively the feeling of wonder.

C.   In contrast to this outward silence, however, there is a powerful activity going on within the participators in the experiences. Inwardly there is the stirring of conjecture about the greatness of the event — of the new vistas opened by the discovery. The contrast of silence and inner speculation is conveyed in the very effective climactic image:

> . . . and all his men
> Looked at each other with a wild surmise —
> Silent, upon a peak in Darien.

D. In the space of fourteen lines Keats covers compactly and effectively the seeker or explorer, the object discovered, the moment of silent awe, and the recognition of and speculation about the enormity of the discovery in the physical and intellectual worlds of man.

The first sentence of paragraph A provides the theme idea of the entire essay, and the second sentence contains the topic sentence of this first paragraph, a division of the theme idea. The details are not merely listed; they are interpreted in relation to the three kinds of explorers, and their symbolical value is discussed in terms of man's discovery. Then the vastness of the discoveries is related to the sense of motion in the poem.

The first paragraph would be a failure if it relied solely on the first two sentences (step one—generalization). It would also fail if it were merely to add to these sentences a list of the explorers (step two—details) as the first version of the paragraph does. The value of the paragraph lies in how it interprets that list and relates it to the topic sentence (step three—interpretation of details).

Paragraph B treats the response to discovery by providing paraphrase and brief quotations. Sentence four extracts the important details in the sonnet, but these have been prepared for by a series of interpretative generalizations in the first three sentences. The rest of the paragraph develops the idea of contrast and repeats and adds details to carry on the interpretation.

In paragraph C the one main detail from the poem is the quotation of the last two and one-half lines of the sonnet. No discussion follows this quotation. However, the image is prepared for by the first two interpretative sentences of the paragraph. To carry on the discussion after the quotation would probably lead to needless repetition.

Throughout the analysis of Keats' sonnet, the three-step procedure is clear. As a result, generalizations are supported by details which do not dominate them. In the details selected and the interpretative comments, there is no evidence of slanting or misreading. By starting with a worth-while theme idea and by developing it with sufficient complexity, the essay avoids the pitfall of superficiality.

Chapter 5

ORGANIZATION

Since an interpretation is essentially the explanation and evaluation of a literary work, it must be written coherently. Just as a poem or a story has its own shape or design, so does the critical essay. Without some kind of design the poem or the interpretation would be incoherent to a reader. Even a story or poem presented in the seemingly chaotic form of stream of consciousness may have a very carefully worked out pattern — a deliberate ordering of disorder. The interpreter of literature, of course, would not write in the stream of consciousness mode. He has to provide his readers with logical patterns of organization, since even the best ideas can be destroyed by incoherent arrangement. Although the outline of an interpretative paper need not stand out like a skeleton spotlighted in a dark corner, the reader should feel that he is being led logically and fluently from one point to the next in an essay.

Clear organization requires meticulous attention to the relationships of parts and details in an essay. Without patient, careful planning, the student will have difficulties. As we have seen in Chapter 2, this planning should be linked to the notes and ideas recorded and, above all, to the theme idea. Once the theme idea is determined, then the process of breaking it down into smaller units can begin; these divisions are the equivalent of the Roman numerals, and occasionally the capital letters, in an outline. In turn, these units must also be subdivided to take care of smaller generalizations and details; these are the Arabic numerals and lower case letters in an outline. In this process of dividing and subdividing, every step is important.

LOSS OF FOCUS

Just as the theme idea is crucial to development of content, so it is also an essential tool in solving problems of organization. If the outline of an essay is carefully arranged in accord with the theme idea, the author of a literary interpretation will not have problems with focus—that is, with sticking to the theme idea with which he started. If the paper is assembled without concern for the central generalization, even if it is an excellent one, or if the theme idea is vague or poorly defined, then the author will invariably lose or blur the focus on his theme idea.

An example of loss of focus is the following student theme on Lardner's "Haircut":

> At first glance, Ring Lardner's story "Haircut" seems to be only for the reader's pleasure. Looking closer, we see that it is a characterization of a small-town barber who devotes part of his time and most of his very limited intelligence to the praise of Jim Kendall. Jim evidently had a warped and bitter outlook on life. He was a practical joker and found his greatest delight in making people unhappy.
>
> I was somewhat amazed at the lack of four-letter words in this story. I find it hard to believe that anyone like the barber could carry on such a "clean" conversation. It might be noted, too, that the time required to read the story is the average length of time for a haircut.
>
> As the barber told Jim's story, he betrayed his own illiteracy and plain lack of intelligence in several ways. His language was probably the most obvious giveaway to his stupidity. [Examples are given.]

The troubles in this theme are due to an unclear conception of the theme idea. The first paragraph simply indicates the nature of the relationship of the barber to Jim, but this glimmer of a theme idea is immediately destroyed in the second paragraph by a series of personal reactions to the story. This second paragraph not only lacks unity but completely obscures the focus.

If the student had started with the following first paragraph, he would have had less difficulty in defining his theme idea and maintaining clear focus:

> In "Haircut" the essential meaning is conveyed to the reader by Lardner's consistent use of irony. There are two

kinds of irony: that associated with the barber's self-revelations and that stemming from the climactic event in his rambling account, the death of Jim.

With this paragraph as a guide, the writer can now concentrate on the irony in the story, and he can look at it from the two closely related points of view suggested in the paragraph. The student writing this second introductory paragraph would be less likely to have difficulty with maintaining a clear focus on his material or with arranging the major parts of his theme.

FAILURE TO USE TRANSITIONS
TO ACHIEVE FOCUS AND FLUENCY

In the construction of expository and analytical essays, transitions are indispensable ingredients. As guides and pointers they help the writer acquire focus. For example, by repetition or careful restatement of key words and phrases, he can point to his theme idea throughout a paper. Transitions are also the tools of fluency — the clear and graceful movement of style, thought, and structure in writing. They provide links within sentences, between sentences, between paragraphs, and between major parts of an essay.

Some of the most commonly used transitions are these:

1) Pronouns as links to their antecedents, the nouns whose places the pronouns take.

2) Purely transitional words and phrases which function solely to point out connections, additions, and alternatives: *however, furthermore, nevertheless, for example, on the other hand,* etc. To these should be added conjunctions, both coordinating and subordinating. Coordinating conjunctions link equal parts of a sentence; they can also operate between sentences — that is, between details or thoughts separated in sentence form. Subordinating conjunctions show the precise relationship between a main clause and the detail or idea subordinated to it.

3) Echo words: key words and phrases directly repeated or reworded — particularly effective in keeping the theme idea or the topic sentence of a paragraph before a reader.

4) Built-in thought progression, such as cause and effect or question and answer, which by logical expectation provides thought links.

5) Transitional paragraphs — short paragraphs which allow

one to summarize what has gone before and to look ahead to the next phase of an essay.

Among the most important problems involving the use of transitions are the thought gap, the movement from paragraph to paragraph, and the need to relate material either to the topic sentence of a paragraph or to the theme idea.

Thought Gap. A particularly prevalent kind of loss of focus within and between sentences is the thought gap, or the missing thought link. In this case the author probably knows what he wants to say but does not provide all the details and ideas necessary. Nor does he present the proper transitions to unite everything clearly. The following two sentences offer a good example of how thought gaps hinder the process of communication and hence blur the focus: "When Mrs. Braggioni washes her husband's feet, an image of Christ is created. The reader suspects that his deceit will continue." A revised version of these sentences might be:

> When Mrs. Braggioni washes her husband's feet, the image of Mary's anointing the feet of Christ is suggested. However, the careful reader has already detected that Braggioni is a fraud, a false savior — in fact, a Judas. The reader also suspects that Braggioni's charity toward his wife is deceitful, for Miss Porter has clearly established that Braggioni has little regard for his wife, or for any woman, and will continue to abandon her whenever he desires.

The revision supplies two missing thoughts: the link to Braggioni as a false savior and the strong suggestion that his wife means very little to him. Words like *However, also,* and *for* supply the necessary transitions between details, and the implications of words like *Christ, savior, Judas,* and *charity* offer further continuity to the revised version. The relationships between all thoughts and details in the paragraph are now clear.

Transitions Between Paragraphs. Since each paragraph in a paper is an important building block in the total structure, it is essential to provide the cement — the transitional links — between them. This tie can be made by relating the topic sentence or the first few sentences at the beginning of each new paragraph to the preceding paragraph or to the theme idea.

When making a transition from one paragraph to another,

the writer can sometimes put the backward-looking element of transition in a subordinate construction and allow the subject matter of the new paragraph to occupy the most prominent place in the sentence. Let us assume that the following sentence begins a new paragraph: "Despite the sensual pleasure derived from his relationship with the Lady, the Knight is led to spiritual despair because the real world lacks faith in his vision." The introductory phrase looks back to the previous paragraph or paragraphs, and the main clause establishes the subject of the new unit, which may, of course, encompass more than one paragraph.

Relevance of Details and Ideas. Sometimes a student will use details and ideas relevant to the topic of a paragraph or of the entire essay but will fail to make that relevance clear to the reader. Such failure will naturally blur the focus and impede the fluency of an essay. Although an author does not have to spell out every implication or every minute step involved in the progression of his thought, he should try to make clear to the reader the relevance of all the material in his essay. In cases where the material is relevant but the writer has not made the relevance clear to his reader, the fault can often be remedied by slight revision or rearrangement. For example, the addition of a brief transition or, if necessary, of a transitional sentence or two pointing more directly to the relationship involved will solve the problem of loss of focus and fluency. We cannot emphasize too much that the reader should not be held responsible for doing the author's work of maintaining focus. At the same time, the author should not insult the reader's intelligence by spelling out the obvious.

Importance of Transitions Demonstrated. To demonstrate how important transitions are in the attainment of clear focus and fluency, let us re-examine the second paragraph of the analysis of Keats' "On First Looking into Chapman's Homer" (p. 57).

(1) It is the response to the discovery which each makes that provides the rich emotional and intellectual impact of wonder or awe. (2) The experience is communicated by Keats through a contrast between the vigor involved as the object of discovery makes its impact and the accompanying response of silence. (3) The object of discovery in each case looms large through the senses. (4) Chapman is pictured

as speaking out *loud and bold*; the planet *swims* suddenly into the vision of the gazer (the pinpointing of a sight object in a vast background); and the enormous Pacific dazzles the *eagle eyes* of Cortez. (5) In contrast to the vigor of the experience — the impact of the object discovered — the response is gentle. (6) Keats' response to Chapman comes through a quiet sense image of breathing serene air. (7) The power in Chapman's clarion ring also contrasts noticeably with the complete outward silence of Cortez and his men. (8) In both instances the observer and participator is struck speechless with awe. (9) In Cortez' case the only sense activity is the gazing of the men at each other. (10) This activity of the men's eyes amid the silence captures effectively the feeling of wonder.

In the first sentence the words *discovery* and *awe* tie the new paragraph to the theme idea stated at the beginning of the essay. These same words, plus the reference to *each*, relate to the discussion of the three kinds of explorers, which is the substance of paragraph one.

Having made these crucial ties, the second paragraph also has to maintain its own movement and structural unity. Sentence two is linked to sentence one by the summarizing word *experience* and by the repetition of *response* and *discovery*. At the same time, the sentence moves forward by introducing the contrast which will govern the rest of the paragraph. Sentence three presents one side of the contrast and repeats the phrase *object of discovery*. The phrase *each case* keeps before the reader the examples of paragraph one; it also leads to sentence four, where the three are discussed. In sentence five comes the contrasting element introduced by the pure transitional phrase *In contrast to* and linked to the rest of the paragraph by the repetition of *experience*, *object*, and *response*. Sentences six and seven offer two examples to support sentence five. The reference to *Chapman* links sentences six and seven, and the verb *contrasts* in sentence seven reinforces the purpose of the paragraph. In sentence eight the words *both instances* and *awe* are signs of focus and fluency. Sentences nine and ten fall together logically and are tied to sentence seven by the reference to *Cortez*. In sentence ten the phrase *This activity* carries the previous sentence forward, as does the emphasis on the words *men's eyes* and *silence*. The final reference to *wonder* keeps alive the theme idea of the essay.

This analysis of the transitions in the paragraph demonstrates how important and how intricate the links between small and large elements in an essay are. Without a conscientious effort to provide these ties, one cannot maintain focus and fluency. At the same time, one should not allow his concentration upon transitions to force him to make them artificial or stilted. The more natural the transitions, the more effective they will be.

POOR ARRANGEMENT OF PARTS

It is possible to make everything in an interpretative essay relate to the theme idea and still have a poorly organized paper. If the large sections, even though related to the central generalization, are arranged poorly, then the effectiveness of the total organization is weakened. If a single paragraph is out of place or incoherent internally, then the organization will also be weak.

Illogical Arrangement of Main Parts. The following theme is ineffectively organized because the main parts are not arranged logically:

> Throughout the adventures of Huckleberry Finn the emphasis is upon freedom — moral freedom, the freedom of physical adventure, and social freedom.
>
> Huck's moral dilemma centers around Jim, the escaped Negro. At first Huck looks down upon Jim just as everyone else has done, but when he recognizes that Jim is a human being who loves his family and who is completely devoted to him, Huck changes his view. Yet in altering his attitude he finds himself in bondage to responsibility — to the need to return Jim to his rightful owner. This conflict between the responsibility he feels and the human attachment to Jim creates for him a moral dilemma. He must decide and free himself of this ethical burden. When he says, "All right, then, I'll *go* to Hell," he decides against society and in favor of humanity. In so doing, however, he ironically feels the weight of guilt upon himself. Through irony, however, Twain has made Huck the only free man, the man capable of innate decision contrary to the dictates of his society.
>
> Huck desires to seek his own life of physical adventure because society impinges on him. The escape from society and his father, the meeting with Jim on the island, and the lengthy trip on the Mississippi River show Huck as the youngster seeking physical freedom. At times he finds him-

self in bondage, especially to the Duke and Dauphin. But the river at least becomes for him a symbol of his free life of adventure.

His freedom is also restricted by the demands of society upon him. Convention requires him to dress properly, to have good table manners, to attend school, to read the Bible, and to go to church. All of these he rejects, and even at the end of the book he is on his way to escape the restrictions of society. He will indeed be a free man.

Although the content of the theme could be considerably improved or at least expanded, we are primarily concerned with the organization. The theme idea is clear enough and actually establishes the arrangement of parts in the paper. It is this arrangement, however, which throws the theme off. A reader looking carefully at the three parts can see a possibility for an order of climax, starting with the least important and moving to the most important section. The paragraph on physical adventure should be placed first, then the section on freedom from the restraints of society, and finally the portion on moral freedom. Moral freedom is so strongly emphasized in the novel that it has to be considered the high point of the theme; yet here it is taken care of first. Everything coming after it is anticlimactic. If the section on moral freedom were put last, then the rest of the theme could be arranged to build up to it. These changes might, of course, involve different transitions, and perhaps the addition of a concluding paragraph, but no major alterations within the paragraphs would be necessary as far as organization is concerned. Even if the content is not changed, the student would have a far better organized theme than the original.

Poor Placement of a Paragraph. Sometimes the general structure of an interpretative essay may be adequate, but one paragraph may be out of place, chiefly because the author has failed to bring related materials together in one section of his paper. Below is an example of this kind of poor placement of a paragraph in a portion of a theme comparing Huck and Tom:

Tom makes games out of all the adventures the two boys get into, whereas Huck responds to them in a much more serious way. In the chapter "We Ambuscade the Arabs," Tom organizes a gang that will rob and kill people. However, the boys, including Huck, eventually get tired of Tom's storybook exploits. During the liberation of Jim, Tom also promotes tactics he has gathered from romantic adventure books. Yet all the while he knows that Jim is actually free. Unaware of this fact, Huck wants to liberate Jim quickly and directly. Jim's freedom is not a game to Huck.

In the book Huck faces several moral dilemmas, whereas Tom does not seem to be aware of such problems. One of Huck's ethical choices involves the freedom of Jim. According to law it was illegal to help a slave to escape. In addition, Huck has been brought up to believe that Negroes are property, not people. As a result of the rattlesnake episode Huck learns that Jim is human. Hence later he has the motive for his decision to protect Jim, even at the expense of his own soul. For Tom there is no concern about the soul.

In the story both boys seem to like adventure — but for different reasons. While traveling down the Mississippi, Huck can escape society and be free of school and church. For this freedom he is willing to face all kinds of adventures. For Tom an adventure is another game — a boy's game of cowboys and Indians.

In this example the content is considerably oversimplified, but the main problem at this point is the failure to bring together the closely related first and third paragraphs. If the third paragraph were moved to the beginning of the selection, the present second paragraph would conclude the paper appropriately. The error in placement of material throws a needless and annoying burden upon the reader and indicates that the author of the essay has not thought out every detail of the structure of his paper.

Confusion Within a Paragraph. Even if the paragraphs are properly placed, poor organization within a paragraph can cause confusion. In a paper dealing with the emotional disturbances of Holden in Salinger's *The Catcher in the Rye*, a student first stressed the poor relationships of Holden with members of his family. After this point was adequately established, the following paragraph appeared in the paper:

Holden has the ability to control his language as he did when he was in the presence of the nuns. Holden is continuously rebelling against his school, sexual, and family environments. The novel ends leaving the reader with doubts as to whether Holden ever will become stable and without emotional problems. And one cannot help wondering whether his sister will continue on the same path, for already she is living in her imaginary world about which she writes.

Not only is this paragraph poorly written, suffering especially from inexact phrasing, but it is a model of internal incoherence which sends the reader jumping aimlessly from point to point. The student has apparently decided to use this paragraph as a catchall for the ideas he did not wish to develop — a kind of miscellany. Yet the lack of clear relevance of the paragraph to the rest of the theme and its loss of internal order and logic practically ruin the entire essay.

THE RUNNING COMMENTARY

A problem of organization which is unique in analytical and interpretative writing occurs because the author is examining a text. Since he is not writing something out of his own experience, he is often tempted to follow the organization of the work being analyzed — to start at the beginning and to plod through the story or poem paragraph by paragraph or stanza by stanza. This procedure prevents his essay from having any individuality of structure. Actually the interpretation is in its own way created and deserves to have its own shape.

If one follows the organization of a poem, drama, or story, he will create difficulties for himself, even if he offers a great deal of interpretation. For example, his running commentary will frequently consist of short, choppy, disconnected thoughts and details — like footnotes on individual lines of a poem. Also, related points will occasionally not be brought together simply because they occur in different places in the text. It is far better for a writer to assemble all the material and interpretation relevant to a phase of his theme idea in one rich paragraph or section of his paper rather than to scatter the details and thoughts throughout the essay.

Following is a running commentary discussing "On First Looking into Chapman's Homer":

In lines 1-3 the image of travel is presented. In line 4 the image is related to literature so that the travel becomes imaginative and not real. Lines 5 and 6 single out one author, Homer, whose value Keats has been told about. In lines 6 and 7 the poet describes the exhilarating experience of acquiring firsthand appreciation of Homer through Chapman's bold interpretation. The first of two comparisons occurs in lines 9 and 10: the poet's discovery is likened to that of an astronomer. The last four lines relate the poet's experience to that of Cortez and his men — the silent, speculative awe that comes from moments of great discoveries.

This running commentary is certainly better than a paraphrase of the poem, for it contains interpretative comments beyond the surface translation of the lines in the paraphrase. However, it is not nearly so rich a synthesis of the poem as is the interpretation on pages 56-58. In the first place, in the running commentary, there is no strongly defined theme idea — just a line-by-line restatement and analysis. Second, the links between words and details in the poem are not presented except as they actually exist in the line-by-line movement of the sonnet. The analysis thus has no individuality, no structure of its own. The main defect, however, is that the commentator has lost sight of the meanings implied in the main experience and those to which it is linked because he has been too intent on each line or group of related lines. Furthermore, he has paid little attention to the techniques Keats used to present the sense of awe.

A professional critic can write a running commentary because he will be aware of the links and will call attention to them, but the running commentary is not recommended for the beginner in literary analysis. At times, of course, one may have to follow the pattern of organization in the work he is discussing. For example, if the topic involves character analysis and the chronology of the story indicates a point of change in the character, then the student would probably have to follow the before and after pattern — without allowing plot details to dominate his analysis of the change. (For an example of an analysis which follows the structure of the literary work, see the discussion of "La Belle Dame sans Merci," pp. 17-19.) The wise student will impose the structure of his essay upon the literary work so that he can acquire the best disciplined organization possible and thus provide a full and coherent journey for the reader.

LACK OF PROPORTION

Another problem which the student writing an interpretative essay may encounter is that of proportion. Proportion is the allotment of space in an essay to ideas and details depending upon their importance. If a theme idea has two equal and related parts, then one should not be treated in a single paragraph and the other in five paragraphs. Nor should a minor point in a section of a paper emerge to dominate that part of the essay. If while organizing or writing an essay, the author finds that certain points have suddenly assumed a new and greater importance, he may have to revise his theme idea to grant them their due significance.

Sometimes lack of proportion will occur because the writer allows his introduction to become too inflated. If, for example, in a theme of eight paragraphs, four are introductory, something is drastically wrong with the proportion. Either the introduction should be pared, or the essay should be extended in order to fulfill the intricate theme idea developed in the first four paragraphs.

The student's need to achieve balance in the structure of an essay is related to solidity of content, for if an important point is played down, then the content as well as the organization will be defective. In order to attain this balance, one cannot resort to slide rules or word counts. He must simply use common sense or at least the guidelines of his own outline.

The loss of proportion or balance in the following theme injures both the organization and content:

In *Moby Dick* two chapters, "The Monkey-Rope" and "The Mat-Maker," provide insight into the theme of fate which runs throughout this vast, cataclysmic story of Ahab's battle with fate. In both chapters Ishmael and Queequeg are performing duties aboard the *Pequod*. Each time the activity leads Ishmael to speculate about man's destiny.

Up to the chapter called "The Mat-Maker," Ishmael has associated fate primarily with the Calvinistic view of predestination. The activity of weaving the mat with Queequeg leads Ishmael to broaden his view of fate. By analogy he links their actions with three aspects of fate. The fixed threads become necessity, for example, the inexorable fact of death or the biological needs of man whereby he sustains himself. Ishmael's own weaving of a thread between the fixed strands he sees as free will—man making his own way or his own decisions in the context of necessity. Queequeg's haphazard striking of the threads with a sword to aid Ishmael's weaving becomes chance—the incidents and experiences which are unpredictable and uncontrollable by the free will. In these events other people, not necessarily the one whose destiny is involved, affect fate. Ishmael thus reasons that of the three — necessity, free will, and chance — chance is the most powerful shaper of man's destiny.

In the novel itself the element of chance — the coinciding of foreboding events and the impact of others — is quite strong. For example, it is chance alone which leads the crewmen to the *Pequod*, and chance that Ahab is their commander. It is Ahab's domination of the boat, his impact upon the men, that creates their destiny. It is also chance that the *Rachel*, spurned by Ahab in its search for a lost son, should rescue the one orphan of the *Pequod*, Ishmael, from the coffin-like lifebuoy which by chance happened to be available to keep him from being swallowed by the mysterious ocean.

In "The Monkey-Rope," the emphasis on the interrelationship between people as part of the definition of chance is startlingly presented through the dangerous activity of Queequeg working on the whale while Ishmael, a rope attached to him, tries to keep his savage friend from being smashed between the whale and the ship.

Thus in two chapters Melville brings to his readers a fascinating analysis of a complicated subject — fate.

This theme lacks proportion because the main emphasis falls upon the chapter "The Mat-Maker," although the theme idea and the conclusion stress two chapters. "The Monkey-Rope" is barely discussed and is almost completely dominated by the second and third paragraphs, even though it holds the climactic position in the theme. "The Mat-Maker" may be the more important chapter, but "The Monkey-Rope" certainly deserves much more discussion to fulfill the prominence announced for it in the theme idea. Both proportion (organization) and content are involved here; the failure is indeed unfortunate, for the first three paragraphs are quite satisfactory in both organization and content. The theme, however, literally runs out of gas.

GOOD ORGANIZATION
DEMONSTRATED AND EXPLAINED

As an example of an interpretative essay which fulfills the basic principles of organization and which concentrates on a single work, examine "The Old Man and the Town" (see the story

"Old Mr. Marblehall" on pp. 179-185) and the analysis of its organization that follows.

The Old Man and the Town

A. (1) In a short story which elaborates no more plot structure than the view of a rich old man taking a walk, Eudora Welty has conveyed, in "Old Mr. Marblehall," a kaleidoscopic portrait of the hostility existing between a town and one of its citizens. (2) By acting as an informal all-knowing point of view in the town, Miss Welty is able to portray both sides and yet sympathize with neither. (3) Though the point of view reports attitudes and fantasies, the reader is not allowed to look too far inside either the town or old Mr. Marblehall. (4) Nevertheless, Miss Welty immerses her readers in a particular environment so that its ambivalent reactions of curiosity and indifference toward Mr. Marblehall are revealed. (5) At the same time the omniscient point of view initiates one into the secret fantasy of a desiccated man who lives out the ticking of the clock only because he contemplates the triumph of shocking his neighbors by the revelation of his double life.

B.   Hovering over this respectable citizen as he walks is the omniscient point of view which reflects the hostility of the public toward old people and the town's curiosity about Marblehall. Toward him there is the hypocritical public remark, "So well preserved!" and the private comment, "One foot in the grave." To represent the curiosity of the town, the point of view gives the reader an observation of the tortured self-conscious wife whom Marblehall had married at sixty. It takes the reader into the somber shadows of his home with its ornate tapestries and heavy furniture. No part of this view is flattering or sympathetic to Mr. Marblehall.

C.   Curiosity and hostility dwell especially on the fact that in old age Mr. Marblehall had married and produced a son, who is now six years old. "The worst of all" declares the point of view, reflecting the town's attitude toward the satyr-like child observed "out walking with old Mr. Marblehall or old Mrs. Marblehall, placing his small booted foot on a little green worm, while they stop and wait on him." And the point of view adds an observation which may indicate the struggle between the public verdict of the town and the secret life of Mr. Marblehall: "Everybody passing by thinks that he looks quite as if he thinks his parents had him just to show they could. You see, it becomes complicated, full of vindictiveness." Perhaps some of the town's inquisitiveness and some of its resentment of the old man may result from its feeling, announced at the beginning of the story, that he "never did anything, never got married until he was sixty."

D. Coexisting with this prying animosity is another aspect of public sentiment portrayed by the all-knowing spokesman — a great indifference toward a figure whom the town feels it has formulated and labeled. Old Mr. Marblehall is merely an insignificant part of the "proper blur" in any traditional or well-ordered town in which no one seems memorable. In the prevailing atmosphere of boredom it would matter little if he were transported for his daily walk to "the East or the West or Kingdom Come." Despite the curiosity about old Mr. Marblehall, no one cares about him as a human being. "He could die, for all they care," the omniscient point of view reveals.

E. Throughout the story the indifference of the town is conveyed by the anonymity implicit in such words describing the town's attitude as *Everybody, People, They,* and *Nobody.* Not even at the end of the story when we see Mr. Marblehall waiting and hoping for the revelation that will crack the placid boredom of the town is the indifference broken. Again the word *Nobody* stands out: "Nobody cares. Not an inhabitant of Natchez, Mississippi, cares if he is deceived by old Mr. Marblehall."

F. It is to destroy this lifelong indifference that Mr. Marblehall projects a shocking second life for himself. From the omniscient perch of observing both the town and Mr. Marblehall, the point of view makes a transition to that second life. The transitional passage underscores the lack of concern:

> But really, nobody pays much attention to his look. He is just like other people to them. He could have easily danced with a troupe of angels in Paradise every night, and they wouldn't have guessed. Nobody is likely to find out that he is leading a double life.

If the town does not find out, the reader does, because the point of view can report everything.

G. The report seems to indicate that the second life is a fantasy constructed by Mr. Marblehall to seek revenge against the indifference of the town. Ironically, he does not know, as the point of view does, that even if his fantasy were real and even if it were revealed, nobody would care.

H. In the fantasy of Marblehall's second life the reader is led again to survey environment, wife, and child. The second environment is a maze and a blur with its streets in which one gets lost, with its "scores of little galleried houses nearly alike," and with its routine and dreary activities of anonymous human beings. The dust that hovers over the community and covers Mr. Marblehall's (Mr. Bird's) zinnias seems to represent the blurring of reality by fantasy. Ironically enough, even in his created second existence old Mr. Marblehall cannot project an exciting escape from the deadening blur of his real life.

I. More indicative of fantasy is the way the point of view describes the second wife. She is compared to "a woodcut of a Bavarian witch, forefinger pointing, with scratches in the air all around her." Although her mouth is very active, she is "static" — so static that the second little boy for a long time "supposed that his mother was totally solid, down to her thick separated ankles." In the description of the first wife — the only wife — one senses human anxiety, but in the caricature of the second wife he sees only the weirdness and bizarre construction of an old man's mind warped by the thought of revenge.

J. Although the children are reported to be alike, the second is smarter. The first is described as follows: "Close up, he has a monkey look, a very penetrating look." About the second, the point of view says, "He finds out things you wouldn't find out. He is a monkey." In the description of the first child the point of view implies the unnatural result of the late marriage. In the blunt and direct statement about the second child lies the implication of fantasy — of Marblehall's transferring and extending the monkey-like nature of the real child to the imagined one. Again the irony of the fantasy is apparent: instead of finding relief for himself, Marblehall creates a second life that is worse than his first.

K. In fact, the point of view seems to relish the fantasy by projecting the monkey-child toward a discovery of his father's duplicity. By so doing, Miss Welty merges the two lives, moving this time from the second to the first.

L. One glaring point of reality identifies and fuses the two worlds — the vivid portrait of old Mr. Marblehall in bed reading the fantastic *Terror Tales*. The first mention of this comes in the public pronouncement of the imagined second wife, whose raucousness probably represents Marblehall's desire to announce his double life to the community. The second reference, including the "stark shadeless bulb," occurs when the point of view hypothetically joins the second life to the first—the real existence. The glaring bulb common to both is reality and reveals that Marblehall's reading about dismembered women and horrendous cult rites has stimulated him to create the fantasy of his second life. Yet that existence is not as horrendous and exciting as the *Terror Tales* because Marblehall's imagination has been permanently deadened by the inescapable reality of Natchez.

M. In projecting his fantasy, he had really wanted to cut through the hostility and yet indifference of the town toward him. This fact becomes clear when the point of view in two places presumes to report Marblehall's feelings. When it is projected that the first child will see the second in the yard, the point of view says, "That would be an interesting thing, a moment of strange telepathies. (Mr. Marblehall can imagine it.)" When the point of view estimates the impact of Marblehall's duplicity, the following sentence qualifies the astonishing and electrifying result: "So thinks self-consoling Mr. Marblehall." Such a statement clearly indicates that Marblehall wants to shock the town out of its complacency.

N. The best evidence, however, comes at the end of the story when the point of view records this observation: ". . . and plunging deeper and deeper he speculates upon some glorious finish, a great explosion of revelations . . . the future." Marblehall even dreams of himself as a butterfly stitching a net. Although this reversal of the roles of hunter and prey—man and butterfly—"doesn't make sense" in a literal way, the dream does make sense psychologically. By seeing himself as a "great blazing butterfly," Marblehall indicates that he wants to attract the eyes of the town. At the same time, by having the butterfly stitch its own net, he reveals an urgent need to have the town trap him in spectacular infamy.

O. Despite his dreams, Marblehall actually lives with the continued animosity and indifference of the town, the naked bulb, his fantasy of a shocking second life, and the obvious failure of his desire for revenge. The people in the community, he thinks, would die if they "knew about his double life." The irony, and the truth, is that they are expecting him to die and do not care if he dies. To this conclusion the omniscient point of view leads the reader.

What are the tools of organization in this interpretative essay?

1) Theme idea: Although the essay is reasonably complex,

the theme idea is established in paragraph A. This stresses the author's point of view, sets up the basic conflict between the town and Marblehall, and introduces the idea of fantasy. In delineating these, the theme idea paragraph provides the basic structure of the essay: the two major parts to be developed are the ambivalent attitude of the town and Mr. Marblehall's response to it.

2) The breakdown of the parts: Paragraph A, the introduction, provides the theme idea. Paragraph O, the conclusion, summarizes the basic ingredients of the analysis and in effect returns to the content of paragraph A. Between A and O come the two major divisions: paragraphs B-F deal with the attitude of the town; paragraphs G-N, with Marblehall's desire for revenge expressed in fantasy. The arrangement is logical in that it first establishes conditions in the community and then Marblehall's response to these. Also, the order is climactic, for Marblehall's fantasy is perhaps the most important aspect of the story.

Within each major division, the smaller parts are clearly organized. Paragraphs B-C express the curiosity and hostility of the town, while paragraphs D-E depict its basic indifference. In the second major division the internal organization is more complex. Paragraph G establishes the purpose of the second division and is like a subtheme idea. In a closely related series of paragraphs (H-J) the fantasy of the second world (environment, wife, child) is examined and in effect related to paragraphs B-C, where Marblehall's first life was discussed. In paragraphs K-L the fusion of Marblehall's two worlds is made. While paragraph L indicates that Marblehall's reading is the cause of the fantasy, the two paragraphs that follow (M and N) offer the psychological reason for it—his desire for revenge.

Each of the paragraphs has its own organizational consistency and progress. Almost every one of them (for example, H-J) is organized around a single important point—a topic sentence. In every paragraph unity and coherence, basic ingredients of organization, are maintained.

3) Maintenance of focus: By reiteration of key words and phrases such as *point of view, town, Mr. Marblehall,* and *fantasy*— or variants of these—the ingredients of the theme idea are always kept before the reader. The clear relationship between the major parts and the logical order within each also make the theme idea unfold fluently and coherently. In other words, the careful construction of the building blocks (the paragraphs) into a clear design automatically keeps the focus on the theme idea.

4) Proportion: The second major division is slightly longer than the first. However, since one has to prove that Marblehall's second world is fantasy, he would need more space for the development of this point. Furthermore, the fact that the town is kept in constant relationship with the analysis in the second part does not allow that division to become dominant. Within each main section, there is a sense of proportion between the parts; for example, in the first division, paragraphs B and C balance paragraphs D and E.

5) Transitions: Continuity is provided by many means in addition to the repetition of key terms relevant to the theme idea (already referred to above in paragraph 3). Within the paragraphs, each sentence is related to the preceding one. In paragraph A, for example, sentence two is linked to sentence one by the repetition of the author's name and by the phrase *both sides*, which recapitulates the two elements of the story described in sentence one. Sentence three picks up *point of view*, referred to in sentence two, and also focuses on the town and Marblehall. The pure transition *Nevertheless* connects sentences three and four. In four, the references to Miss Welty and the emphasis on the town's attitude provide continuity. In sentence five, the transitional phrase *At the same time* is the immediate link; in addition, reference to the point of view and the stress on Marblehall's reaction to the town connect this sentence very closely to the others in the paragraph. This same kind of analysis of the transitions connecting sentences could be made for each paragraph in the essay.

The transitions between paragraphs also help a reader. For example, in paragraph C the repetition of the words *curiosity* and *hostility* pick up the main point of paragraph B and identify it with Marblehall's child. In paragraph D the reference to *this prying animosity* goes back to paragraph C, and the phrase *another aspect* foreshadows the new point to be made about the town's attitude. The phrase *More indicative of fantasy* in paragraph I shows that the substance of this paragraph is being compared to that of paragraph H. One should note that the first sentence of paragraph H establishes the organization of three paragraphs (H-J) and hence allows the reader to make the transitions from one to the other easily. Every paragraph is linked to units before and after it.

Two of the paragraphs are mainly transitional. Paragraph F stresses the attitude of the town and moves the reader toward the secret life of Marblehall. In effect, this paragraph emphasizes

Miss Welty's own transition in her story. Paragraph G stems from F and sets up the main point of the next section of the paper—Marblehall's fantasy.

Thus almost every kind of transitional device available to a writer is used in this essay to provide fluency of movement. This fluency, coupled with a well-defined idea, careful arrangement of all parts, and maintenance of clear focus, offers a pattern of organization that any reader can profitably follow.

Obviously the tight control over the material in this essay shows that the author knew what he was doing and that he planned every step carefully before he wrote the selection. While he wrote it, he was conscious of the responsibility of providing his readers with clear and meaningful guidelines of organization.

ORGANIZATION OF A COMPARISON THEME

At times the student may be asked to write a theme in which he will have to deal with two literary works in relation to a theme idea. It is possible to face a similar problem when dealing with only one poem or story—for example, a comparison of two characters. The comparison theme, which would include contrast, poses serious problems of organization. Once the student has selected his theme idea, there are at least three general ways to proceed.

The first way concentrates on each of the works separately and then links them in a climactic section of the paper. The outline for such an approach would look something like this:

Introduction—theme idea
  I. First Work as related to the theme idea
 II. Second Work as related to the theme idea
III. Synthesis—The comparison of the two works; the generalizations drawn from these comparisons can also partially serve as a summary.

This approach, if carefully handled, can be successful, but it establishes three barriers. First, the reader is forced to bear the burden of remembering parts I and II so that the synthesis can be intelligible to him. Second, it will be impossible in part III to avoid the repetition of ideas and possibly details already dealt with. If the repetition becomes too prominent, then the paper will seem to be padded. Since repetition is already a problem, this kind of pattern should not include a summary. A third disadvantage is that, because comparisons are made after the substance of each work has been discussed, the organization in part III may be choppy and disjointed, like a running commentary on one's own theme.

Another approach, after the student has clearly defined his central generalization, is to organize the material in categories of similarities and differences. A general outline using this approach would be:

Introduction — theme idea
    I. Similarities
        A. First Similarity
            1. First Work
            2. Second Work
        B. Second Similarity
            1. First Work
            2. Second Work
   II. Differences
        A. First Difference
            1. First Work
            2. Second Work
        B. Second Difference
            1. First Work
            2. Second Work
  III. Summary

In this approach the student may have material which he cannot clearly classify. For example, if one work stresses a point and the other does not, the comparison is one-sided and hence seemingly absent. Actually this problem can be placed under differences. If the material cannot be classified under either similarities or differences, then it probably is irrelevant to the theme idea and should be omitted.

A very effective way to organize a comparison theme is to build the essay not around the works themselves or around their similarities and differences, but around the theme idea. If that statement is complex enough, it can be broken into smaller generalizations which can be carefully arranged as follows:

Introduction — theme idea
    I. Point A relevant to the theme idea
        A. First Work

           B.   Second Work
           C.   Synthesis of the section [This may run concurrently
               with A and B; it does not have to be a separate step.]
   II. Point B relevant to the theme idea
           A.   First Work
           B.   Second Work
           C.   Synthesis of the section
  III. Summary

No matter which pattern of organization a student chooses for his comparison theme, he must be careful to keep his plan clear for the reader. The opportunities for chaotic organization are literally doubled in the comparison theme.

As an example of the third kind of organization of a theme of comparison, let us examine an essay comparing the Knight in "La Belle Dame" (pp. 14-16) and the narrator in Delmore Schwartz' "The Heavy Bear" (pp. 2-3). The essay will explore the following theme idea: "The sensual and emotional experiences of the Knight in 'La Belle Dame sans Merci' and of the narrator in 'The Heavy Bear' lead to a mood of despair because of the harsh realities of life and man's nature." Instead of discussing each poem separately or basing the organization on similarities and differences, the essay breaks the theme idea into smaller generalizations which are then used as the main sections of organization. The outline would be thus:

Introduction — theme idea
    I. Experiences emphasizing senses and the sensual
        A.   "La Belle Dame" — great emphasis on sense experi-
            ence, but also on grace and beauty
        B.   "The Heavy Bear" — highly sensual and sexual;
            makes appetite gross and clumsy
   II. Conflict with reality
        A.   "La Belle Dame" — reality versus an ideal beauty,
            derived through the supernatural Lady
        B.   "The Heavy Bear" — reality versus the ideal of pure
            love (the spirit)
  III. Results of the experiences
        A.   "La Belle Dame" — despair of the Knight caused by
            forces beyond himself
         B.   "The Heavy Bear" — perplexity and despair of the
            narrator because of inability to control sensuality
            and emotions within himself

C. Points in both poems related to the sense of despair
    1. Image of sleep and despair
    2. Universality of central figure of despair
Conclusion

Comparison of "La Belle Dame" and "The Heavy Bear"

The sensual and emotional experiences of the Knight in "La Belle Dame sans Merci" and of the narrator in "The Heavy Bear" lead to a mood of despair because of the harsh realities of life and of man's nature.

Both poems emphasize the power of experiences based on the senses or on sensuality. In "La Belle Dame," the relationship with the Lady is beautiful, graceful, and seductive. The details describing the Lady and her actions emphasize the Knight's fascination with her; in fact, he is so absorbed by her that he can see nothing else *all day long*. Every one of his senses is engaged: sight, sound, smell, taste, and touch. Yet these are not ordinary sense experiences, for the *wild wild eyes* and the strange language of the woman make her beauty and appeal seem extraordinary, indeed, beyond real experience.

In "The Heavy Bear," on the other hand, the senses and emotions are vividly and realistically distorted and unpleasant; they are far from graceful, beautiful, and exotic. The senses in effect become the uncontrollable appetites of man, particularly his sensuality. The bear is the symbol of man's inner urges or appetites. The animal's brutish, heavy, lumbering nature and his need for candy, honey, and sugar connote the essential crudeness and irrepressibility of man's drives and emotions. Of these, the grossness of man's sexual nature is most emphasized, especially in the crude embrace of the beloved one.

The world of the senses in "La Belle Dame" is idealized; it becomes a vision of beauty which lies beyond the physical but which is attainable through the senses. This visionary quality of the Knight's experience is conveyed by the Lady. She is beyond reality, an inhabitant of a supernatural kingdom. She is described as *a faery child*, who sings a *faery's song*. The grot, the center of her supernatural existence, is an *elfin grot*. The Knight, then, is pursuing something outside the real world of the warring Kings and Princes, whose skepticism shatters his pursuit of ideal beauty and returns him to the spiritual despair of the cold hill's side—the despair which the observer so graphically sees in the Knight's face.

In "The Heavy Bear," the narrator is not pursuing ideal beauty represented in a supernatural female form. He seems to be plagued all too powerfully and persistently by the nagging reality of *belly and bone*, by the drives of sexual appetite and fierce emotion. Yet in this poem there is an implied ideal which establishes a contrast, just as the real and the ideal collide in "La Belle Dame." The implied ideal of Schwartz' poem involves love—the pure love of the beloved which can be inferred in the last stanza. The narrator's better self, his spirit, is aware of the grossness of the sexual attraction to the *very dear,* but the reality of that attraction overpowers the recognition of the purity of love. As the narrator says, the bear is a "stupid clown of the spirit's motives." Although this ideal is perhaps not as strongly portrayed as is the vision of beauty in "La Belle Dame," it is in Schwartz' poem a basic part of the conflict between the reality of appetite and the pure motives of the spirit.

In both poems the conflicts lead to perplexity and despair in the Knight and in the first person narrator. The Knight's despair comes because of the disillusionment that attends the failure of the projection of his better self—the vision of ideal beauty. The lack of faith in that vision by the warriors of the real world destroys the ideal. The Knight then is the victim of forces outside the vision. On the other hand, the narrator of Schwartz' poem is the victim of forces within himself—his uncontrollable appetites.

In both poems, interestingly enough, the reality which creates despair comes in images of sleep. The Knight's seemingly comfortable sleep in the arms of the Lady is destroyed by the dream of the princes and warriors. In stanza two of Schwartz' poem, an ominous note of fear of the dark extremes of appetite and of the ultimate extinction of the *quivering meat* is conveyed in the nighttime inner turbulence of the heavy bear, who sleeps with the narrator, breathing heavily at his side.

Even more ominous is the implication of the universality of the experiences depicted in each poem. The Knight could be Everyman failing in the pursuit of ideal beauty, although Keats never makes an explicit statement of the symbol. Schwartz, on the other hand, directly expands his major symbol, the bear, in the last two lines: "Amid the hundred million of his kind, / The scrimmage of appetite everywhere."

Although the two poems were written well over a century apart and although the poets approach their subjects quite differently, they make similar comments on the bitter realities of human experience.

Chapter 6

MATTERS OF STYLE

Even if a student defines a theme idea perceptively, provides some excellent ideas and details, and organizes his essay logically, he may still mar his essay by stylistic lapses. One cannot present ideas effectively unless he expresses them clearly. Because we cannot go into every stylistic problem a student may confront, we shall concentrate on four difficulties common in themes of literary analysis: incoherent sentence structure, wordiness, jargon, and poor integration of quotations.

In each of these problems, communication between the author and his readers is deeply involved. If at any time a student breaks down or impedes this process, he is in effect defeating his main purpose in writing his theme—to explain his ideas and the details he chooses to support them. If such breakdowns are too frequent, then the essay becomes worthless.

INCOHERENT SENTENCE STRUCTURE

In any standard composition book, numerous errors in sentence structure are discussed. Here we shall simply provide some examples of faulty sentence structure that destroy communication.

In a theme on Oedipus, a student carelessly included the two following sentences:

The tragic flaw being the eruption of Oedipus' emotions upon the revelation and the tragedy complete with the suicide of his wife and the piercing of his eyes with his own two hands.

The [Oedipus] complex being, where the father is hated by his son and love for his mother.

A reader would have great difficulty with both of these sentences. Both are fragmentary; but, although some fragments can be understood, these examples have other difficulties which impair communication. In the first sentence, the two phases of the tragedy are not carefully distinguished or emphasized. In the second, a lack of parallelism (unequal grammatical and structural parts connected by a coordinating conjunction) makes the explanation of the Oedipus complex incomprehensible.

When sentences are garbled, it is difficult to determine the author's meaning. However, we shall try to rewrite the two sentences in order to provide clear statements:

Oedipus' tragic flaw can be seen during his emotional eruption when his unintentional sins are revealed. The tragedy is complete when Jocasta commits suicide and Oedipus pierces out his own eyes.

The Oedipus complex involves hatred of one's father and love for one's mother.

A sentence from a student's theme on Joseph Conrad's *Typhoon* further demonstrates dramatically how faulty sentence structure and inexact phrasing impede communication:

This is so contrary to Jukes' belief that a man who has experienced storms and knows about them is qualified to write such a book, and that this man cannot be considered in error that Jukes believes the captain to be stupid.

This sentence contains a clumsy piling-up of *that* clauses, and, more important, the structure is so completely confused that the meaning is almost unintelligible. What the student may have been thinking about was Captain MacWhirr's refusal to abide by the comments about typhoons in a book, and Jukes' reaction to the Captain's literal-mindedness. However, the sentence structure and the phrasing employed by the writer do not convey the meaning clearly. By adding a detail or two, one might communicate the original idea in two sentences:

Jukes believes that one who has experienced storms is qualified to write about them and cannot be considered wrong, especially by the Captain, who has never faced a typhoon before. Because of the Captain's reaction to the book, Jukes feels that he is stupid.

WORDINESS

Wordiness can also destroy the fluency of a sentence and slow down the process of communication. Although a reader may be able to derive the author's meaning, he will definitely be irritated by the author's carelessness and by the need to cut through the verbiage. Here we shall be concerned with three kinds of wordiness: (1) stating a concept in more words than are necessary; (2) needlessly repeating one idea or detail; and (3) overemphasizing an already obvious point by piling up details.

Because a student may not have a clear conception of a sentence—the grammatical functions and relationships of its parts—he will sometimes use more words than necessary. If he has a poor vocabulary or if his word sense is based on bad habits and poor logical processes, he is likely to be long-winded. No matter what causes wordiness, it can invariably be correlated with clumsiness. The following twenty-seven-word sentence from a student theme is a good example: "In all of the adventures that the two boys get into, Tom makes a game out of it and Huck takes it in a more serious way."

There are several problems here. First, the student has no clear view of the structure; hence he doubles back on himself by using the pronoun *it* (ungrammatically) when actually he need not have used the word at all. In addition, his word sense is inflated; for *In all of the adventures that the two boys get into* can be converted to *In their adventures* (three words for eleven). In fact, to avoid clumsiness and wordiness one would have to redirect the focus of the sentence as follows: "Tom makes all of their adventures into games, whereas Huck responds in a more serious way" (sixteen words instead of twenty-seven). Obviously, if a theme has several or many such wordy sentences, the reader will be slowed down considerably—or even stopped entirely.

The same student theme provides an example of needless repetition of one idea or detail. One paragraph contained the following statements (taken out of the context of details): "Tom has a mania to turn everything into a storybook adventure. . . . Tom's storybook description of their exploits has worn off. Tom is continually promoting ideas which he has picked up in a book. . . . These plans involve many things that he has picked out of a book. . . ." A reader observing these useless repetitions within one paragraph is likely to stop reading. Repetition can be effective if used for stylistic effect, for transitions, or for maintenance of focus on a theme idea. In the example above, however, there is no justification for the repetition of a simple point.

Sometimes a student will be wordy without using excessive words or repeating the same point or details. In fact, he can write a paragraph or section of his paper correctly but still impede his reader by simply piling up numerous details to support a point so obvious to the reader that the words seem wasted and merely induce a feeling of impatience for the theme to move to more significant and complex matters. Such an elaboration of the obvious is represented in the following passage:

> [One of Huck's basic qualities is a love of playing tricks.] Jim seemed to be the primary target of Huck's trickplaying, as demonstrated by the placing of the dead rattlesnake in Jim's bed in the cavern. "I killed him and curled him up on the foot of Jim's blanket ever so natural, thinking there'd be some fun when Jim found him there." Also in the episode where Huck and Jim get separated in the fog, Huck returns to the raft, finds Jim asleep, and so decides to play as if he (Huck) had been there all along and as if Jim must have been just having a nightmare.
>
> Aunt Sally doesn't escape the tricks of Huck either, as shown in the "spoon episode" with Tom. This is the time when Huck slid the spoon up his sleeve, Tom would count it, Huck would put the spoon back, Tom would recount to Aunt Sally, etc., with resulting confusion as to whether there were actually nine or ten spoons present.

JARGON

The use of jargon drawn from a specialized vocabulary can frequently lead to wordiness and unintelligibility. Such an effect is ironical because many people justify the specialized vocabulary of their fields on the ground that it saves time. A technical term, they argue, can say in a few words what would require many more words from the layman. In many cases this argument is valid. Yet anyone who has read much literary criticism or many psychological and sociological studies knows that the overuse of technical terms, or jargon, is not timesaving. More probably, it becomes a display of rhetoric that creates confusion rather than light.

In literary criticism, the worst kind of jargon occurs when the critic adds to his own arsenal of special words technical terms adopted from other languages or from other areas of study. Even in a brilliant book like Northrop Frye's *Anatomy of Criticism*, one encounters indecipherable sentences such as the following: "Alchemical symbolism takes the ouroboros and the hermaphrodite *(res bina)*, as well as the traditional romantic dragon, in this redemptive context."[1] Even a knowledgeable reader would have trouble with this sentence — in or out of context.

A dramatic example of inflated language stemming from jargon is offered by the following pair of sentences, one of which was concocted by a teacher trying to deflate the pompous language used by some of his students. The other sentence comes from the King James version of the Bible, whose simple eloquence has exercised great influence upon English style in prose and poetry.

> As a result of the accultural inequities in his natural habitat and as a result of the natural drives that subconsciously motivate all men, Jesus initiated the complex physiological mechanism which eventuated in salted water's seeping through his tear ducts.

> JESUS WEPT.

A student encountering the first sentence will realize that the author is trying to show off a vocabulary garnered in psychology and sociology classes. The reader will easily detect the inflation of verbiage and will quickly determine that the Bible is far more interesting than the theme written about it.

POOR INTEGRATION OF QUOTATIONS

Another way to impede communication between a writer and his reader is failure to integrate quotations skillfully. Since the author of a literary interpretation will occasionally use quotations from the work being analyzed in order to support his points, he must know how to fuse them into his own text. When the quotation is not gracefully linked to what comes before and after, then the reader is forced to make leaps to and from it. In the following passage from a theme on *Darkness at Noon*, the quotation is not adequately integrated:

1. Northrop Frye, *Anatomy of Criticism* (Princeton, 1957), p. 157.

Another sacrifice was evident in the flashback to Arlova and her intimate affair with Rubashov. "Only the earrings now lay flat on the pillow. *Her eyes* had the same expression as ever, when she pronounced that sentence which could no more leave Rubashov's memory than the folded hands of the 'Pieta'."

In this example the sentence introducing the quotation does not clearly place the flashback in Rubashov's mind. Hence the reader is startled when he has to leap from a sacrifice to the earrings in the quotation. The following introductory sentence would prepare the reader for the quotation: "Rubashov's guilt-ridden mind is haunted by images and thoughts of Arlova: [Quotation]."

Another example of poor integration of quotations occurs in a student theme on D. H. Lawrence's "The Captain's Doll":

Again we are told about the "friendly" relationship of Alexander to his wife. It seems almost as if he treats her as a doll, breakable, but not to be hurt for anything. "We're very good friends. Why, we've been friends for eighteen years — we've been married seventeen. Oh, she's a nice little woman. I don't want to hurt her feelings."

The quotation here jars the reader because the sentence before it is an inadequate preparation. In this case, the integration could easily be made by providing this preface: "Explaining his relationship with his wife, Alexander says to Hannele, 'We're very good friends.' [etc.]"

Short quotations are properly integrated when they fit smoothly into the student's sentence. The working-in of a quoted phrase or even an independent thought can usually be taken care of. In most such cases, especially when words or phrases are integrated, the three ellipses (...) designating an omission would not be used either before or after the quotation. This example demonstrates the fusion of a short quotation with the author's sentence: "'The worst of all' declares the point of view, reflecting the town's attitude toward the satyr-like child observed 'out walking with old Mr. Marblehall or old Mrs. Marblehall, placing his small booted foot on a little green worm, while they stop and wait on him.' " The quoted portion fits in both grammatically and structurally.

Sometimes, of course, a short quotation can be introduced in a more formal way by means of the phrase *as follows* or *the following.* At times a very brief prepositional introduction can prepare the reader for a short quotation, as in the following: "According to Ishmael, 'That unsounded ocean you gasp in, is life; these sharks, your foes; those spades, your friends; and what between sharks and spades you are in a sad pickle and peril, poor lad.'"

Long quotations are especially troublesome. Quotations of more than three lines are usually set off from the text and single-spaced, but this procedure does not guarantee integration of the quotation. If the long quotation is not in some way linked to what precedes it, the reader will become lost. The author can integrate long quotations in two ways. He can provide an artificial transitional phrase, clause, or sentence. For example, in order to demonstrate the point of a paragraph in an essay on William Faulkner, Robert Penn Warren introduced his illustrative quotation in this way: "Take, for instance, the passage from 'The Bear': [passage quoted]." The writer should, however, introduce the quotation naturally, if possible. The one long quotation (paragraph F) in the essay "The Old Man and the Town" (pp. 72-75) is introduced without artificial devices: "The transitional passage underscores the lack of concern: [passage quoted]." Here the introduction even relates the quotation to the content of the previous two paragraphs.

There are numerous ways to integrate quotations, and a writer must use every means possible to fuse them coherently and fluently into his text. If he does not, he will mar the style of his essay and impede communication.

Chapter 7

RESEARCH

AND THE LITERARY INTERPRETATION

The major emphasis in this book thus far has been upon the interpretation of literary works without the use of research. However, even to an intrinsic examination of a work, a student must bring some knowledge outside the text. His general background of information, knowledge acquired through his college courses in such subjects as psychology and history or through independent reading, his understanding of literary terms or of allusions—all these represent a capital fund from which he can draw to enrich his interpretation. But the use of such sources may not require documentation by means of footnotes.

Frequently, however, the student will recognize that his knowledge is insufficient to cope with a literary work, or he will be given specific writing assignments involving the relationship of research to literature. In these cases, he cannot rely on what he has already learned in classes; he will have to use the resources of the library. An example of such a project would be a study to determine by investigation of biographical materials whether Keats' moods during the time "La Belle Dame" was written had anything to do with the sense of despair in the poem.

Projects of this sort are quite different from research essays presenting pure biography, literary history, or the like, although these, of course, can be very useful and meaningful. The linking of research to interpretation poses special problems for the writer, because it is probably easier to write a paper on pure biography than to make biographical information a basic part of an interpretation of a poem, story, or play. It is also easy to unreel facts collected in research and to forget about or bury the literary work being analyzed.

A student may ask, "How much research should I put into my interpretative essay?" Actually it is impossible to answer this question because the degree of balance between the research material and the interpretation derived from intrinsic analysis depends entirely upon the individual project and upon the requirements of the instructor's assignment. In some cases the research data may simply be a platform on which to build an interpretation. In other instances, the research may be more dominant. Although the question cannot be dogmatically answered, the student should recognize that some basic principles are involved. First, if the facts garnered from research substitute for interpretation, then the resulting essay will be history or biography rather than an interpretation fusing analysis of the work with information derived from research. Second, if the research is relevant to the interpretation being offered, it should be carefully integrated into the essay.

If one accepts these basic principles, he also needs to recognize that the special combination being discussed here is similar to, as well as different from, research he may do in other courses. His procedure in assembling and documenting data will be like that which he would employ in any kind of research. In compiling his material, the student will have to take notes, preferably on cards, on primary sources—the literary works themselves or comments of an author about his own art, for example—and on secondary sources, which constitute materials written about the works and their authors. While taking his notes, he must carefully avoid adhering too closely to the wording of his sources, unless, of course, he is quoting directly from them. As he digests and arranges his material, he must also evaluate the validity of his sources. If, for example, he is discussing criticism of an author or of a specific literary work, he must deal cautiously with comments made by a bitter foe of the author whose text is being examined. Careful study of his notes during this pre-writing period will be invaluable to the student who wishes to synthesize his material and to organize it into a good essay. It will assist him in directing his paper toward a clear statement of theme idea and in forming an outline for his essay. He should try to transcribe his brief and disjointed notes into a workable, coherent draft, and then, after careful scrutiny of it, he ought to rearrange and reword those portions of his essay which do not contribute to his purpose. During his final attempt to blend his material coherently into a finished paper, he should recheck his references to see that he is being accurate in referring to his sources and also to see that he has not, inadvertently, echoed his reading without giving either exact quotations or footnote credit.

In his essay he will follow standard procedures of documentation: footnotes and bibliography may be necessary so that a reader can determine what material was obtained from research. For stylistic matters of formal documentation, particularly footnote and bibliography forms, the *MLA Style Sheet* and *A Manual of Style* (University of Chicago Press) are useful. If informal documentation is permissible, the student can refer to his sources in the body of his paper. An example would be, "According to Arthur Hobson Quinn in his biography *Edgar Allan Poe*," etc.

In addition to note-taking and documentation, the student must be acutely aware of all the problems of writing a literary interpretation discussed in Chapters 2 through 6. Since the research essay may be longer and more complicated than other papers, he should be especially careful about limiting his subject. Without a clearly defined and limited purpose, one will flounder through every stage of a research paper. Because he has the added burden of linking research data to an interpretation, he ought to be most attentive to solidity of content, organization, and correctness and clarity of expression.

In selecting a subject for a paper combining literary analysis with research, the student has an amazingly wide range of choice. Some of the possible areas for research related to literary interpretation might be summarized thus:

1)   Textual criticism: the establishing of the best possible text of a work or of the author's final revision. (*Examples:* The Revisions of "To Helen," The Revisions of "La Belle Dame.")

2)   The relationship of one work by an author to his other writings: the tracing of a theme and/or technique; the study of the artistic or intellectual development of the author; and evaluation of the body of his work — possibly selected. (*Examples:* The Ironic Style of Katherine Anne Porter, Keats and the Pursuit of Beauty, Sense of Place in Welty's Stories.)

3)   Biography: the relevance of autobiography to a literary work; also the relationship of biographical facts. (*Examples:* "La Belle Dame," A Study of Keats' Despair; Poe's Helens: Reality and Imagination; Autobiography in Selected Works of Katherine Anne Porter.)

4)   The creative process, particularly the author's intention in a given work, as shown in sources used by the author, in his journals and letters, and in changes which he made in various

published versions of the work under examination. (*Examples:* The Source of Shakespeare's *Othello;* "The Ambitious Guest": from Fact to Fiction; The Evolution of *What Maisie Knew*.)

5) The relationship of the work to literary theory, especially to the author's concept of his art. *(Examples:* Arthur Miller's Concept of Tragedy in *Death of a Salesman,* Poe's Concept of Poetry as Applied to the Lyric "To Helen," Hawthorne's Concept of the Romance and *The Scarlet Letter*.)

6) The impact of an author's times on his work, including the influences of contemporaries upon him. *(Examples:* Hemingway's *The Sun Also Rises* and the Waste Land, *Huckleberry Finn* as a Reflection of Its Era, Whitman's Use of the Civil War in His Poetry.)

7) The relationship of a work to its genre or to traditions of content and style. (*Examples:* Keats' Use of the Sonnet Form, Is *Huckleberry Finn* a Picaresque Novel? The Ballad Tradition and "La Belle Dame.")

8) The relationship of a work or works to subject areas such as semantics, psychology, folklore, myth, religion, anthropology, history, sociology, economics, political science, science, philosophy, and fine arts. (*Examples:* Freud and "The Heavy Bear," The Effect of Science on Matthew Arnold's "Dover Beach," Modern Russian History and *Darkness at Noon*.)

9) Comparative literary study: the relationships between works, between authors, and also between the works and movements of different national cultures. (*Examples:* Poe's Influence on Baudelaire [some phase], Gothic Elements in Hawthorne's Fiction, Strindberg's Impact on Eugene O'Neill.)

10) The body of criticism of an author or of a specific literary work. (*Examples:* An Evaluation of Interpretations of Melville's Whale, Interpretations of Hester in *The Scarlet Letter,* Interpretations of "Flowering Judas," Interpretations of Shakespeare's Sonnet 73.)

Some of these areas are highly specialized and probably more suitable for advanced students of literature, but in the list there are several categories of investigation which can be pursued profitably by anyone asked to relate research to literary analysis. Here we shall be concerned with the problems a beginning student might encounter in three promising areas: biography as related to interpretation (3 above); criticism of a given work or author in relation to one's own analysis (10 above); and the study of the creative process as shown in a search for the author's intention and development of his purpose (4 above).

BIOGRAPHY
AND LITERARY INTERPRETATION

For some authors it is almost necessary to relate biography to interpretation. If the author is intensely autobiographical, if he is transmuting into imaginative expression the reality of his experience, a knowledge of his life may help one to determine guidelines of interpretation or even of analysis of artistry. A good example of such an author is Eugene O'Neill. Although his plays can stand on their own achievement, some of them become even more meaningful in the context of his life.

Since many students wish to learn more about a writer whose work attracts them, this is an area toward which students doing research in relation to literature naturally gravitate. However, certain cautions are necessary for a student embarking on such a library investigation. First and foremost, he must recognize that the biographical data he discovers should be used only to illuminate or interpret the work or works being examined. Concentration on biography should not provide a substitute approach to those who have trouble interpreting a literary text. The literary student should use only that biographical detail which will help him understand the meaning and art of a poem or story; otherwise, no substantial interpretation — either analysis or evaluation of literary work — will result.

Just as one can ignore a literary text and concentrate on biography, so one can use the work as a source of biographical information. Again the emphasis would be misplaced. For example, so little is known about Shakespeare's intimate thoughts and feelings that many tend to use his poetry to discover the man. Edgar Allan Poe has been frequently placed on the psychoanalyst's couch by means of his stories. Even though an author may be highly neurotic or even psychotic, there are dangers in establishing a direct equation between the man and his works. It is absurd, for instance, to assume that every disturbed narrator in Poe's stories is a representation of some phase of his creator's psyche. Instead of using literature as a source of biography, the student should reverse the procedure and allow biographical investigation to help him understand the meaning and art of a literary creation.

A final problem occurs when one's response to the life, ideas, or personality of an author prevents him from studying the literary production objectively. Actually one should maintain objectivity as a scientist would, pronouncing impartially according to criteria clearly defined to himself and to his reader. All too often the partialities and prejudices, perhaps unconscious, of a student influence the tone and content of his essay. Authors like John Milton, Robinson Jeffers, Ezra Pound, and T. S. Eliot have been rejected or treated unfairly by those who do not like them. Even classics like Shakespeare's *The Merchant of Venice* and Twain's *The Adventures of Huckleberry Finn* have been condemned because minority groups do not care for the characterizations of Shylock and Jim. On the other hand, many undistinguished or minor writers and works have been overestimated by students whose intensive exploration of biography caused undue devotion. When one studies a writer so thoroughly, or when one is congenial with his ideas, he may exaggerate the literary value of his idol. To avoid the affective fallacy, a student must maintain objectivity, whether he detests or admires the writer whose life and work he is examining.

To demonstrate some of the difficulties involved in relating biography to literary interpretation, a portion of an essay on Poe's "To Helen" follows:

Helen: Legend or Reality?

Poe claimed that he wrote "To Helen" in "earliest boyhood" and that he was inspired by Mrs. Jane Stith Craig Stanard, mother of his friend Robert.[1] To Poe, Mrs. Stanard was "the first, purely ideal love of [his] soul. . . ."[2] Despite these claims by Poe, there is some dispute concerning the identity of Helen and the relevance of the real-life woman to interpretation of the poem.

Although he does not believe that Poe wrote the poem in "earliest boyhood," Arthur Hobson Quinn does accept Mrs. Stanard as the model of Helen. He interprets the words "regions which are Holy Land" as reference either to Greece or Rome, "or to the surroundings of Mrs. Stanard, who was to [Poe] a sacred presence."[3]

Others say that Mrs. Frances Keeling Allan, Poe's foster mother, could have been the prototype of Helen. Poe, some critics

1. Arthur Hobson Quinn, *Edgar Allan Poe* (New York, 1942), pp. 85-86, 177-178.
2. Poe to Sarah Helen Whitman, October 1, 1848. *The Letters of Edgar Allan Poe*, ed. John Ward Ostrom (Cambridge, Mass., 1948), II, 385.
3. Quinn, p. 179. For others who accept Mrs. Stanard as the original inspiration, see *The Selected Poetry and Prose of Edgar Allan Poe*, ed. T. O. Mabbott (New York, 1951), p. 408, and Edward D. Snyder, "Poe's Nicean Barks," *Classical Journal*, XLVIII (February, 1953), 159.

claim, "might be here celebrating Mrs. Allan's coming with a lamp in her hand to kiss him goodnight," or he may have caught "in the poem a memory of Mrs. Allan framed in a window niche and reading a letter."[4]

Two students of Poe have suggested that the poem is a composite portrait of two women, Mrs. Stanard and Mrs. Allan. Paull F. Baum feels that Mrs. Stanard may have first inspired the lyric but that, by the time it was published in 1831, Mrs. Allan had become a part of the inspiration.[5] To Hervey Allen, the same composite also includes "the abstract longing for the perfect Belovéd common to all young men."[6]

Some of the critics and biographers, particularly Baum, admit that the evidence for any of these interpretations is speculative, yet the attempts to identify Helen with somebody other than Helen of Troy persist.

For example, the case for Mrs. Stanard as the model rests largely on evidence supplied by Mrs. Helen Whitman, with whom Poe later passionately identified the poem "To Helen," as well as with his earlier relationship with Mrs. Stanard.[7] Yet this evidence is so confusing that controversy is even stirred up about how many times Poe actually saw Mrs. Stanard.[8] [The essay continues the examination of the case for Mrs. Stanard and then moves to other possibilities.]

The approach demonstrated above raises certain important questions. Is it really a literary interpretation? There seems to be so much concentration on the arguments of the students of Poe and on straightening out the confusing contradictions that there is very little direct relationship of facts collected in research to the actual text of the poem. In paragraphs two and three there is attention to the text; however, these instances indicate that the poem is being used to determine who the model is. Literary interpretation in effect gets buried.

Another question arises: Can the research material help one interpret the poem? In his *Poe, A Critical Study*, Edward Davidson says that the identification of Helen (other than Helen of Troy) does not matter to anyone interested in analyzing the poem. Even though this view may be valid, one can argue that the research data may be useful. The facts presented by Quinn,

4. Edward H. Davidson, *Poe, A Critical Study* (Cambridge, Mass., 1957), p. 32.
5. Paull F. Baum, "Poe's 'To Helen,'" *Modern Language Notes*, LXIV (May, 1949), 295.
6. Hervey Allen, *Israfel* (New York, 1927), I, 308.
7. *Letters*, II, 385-386.
8. Quinn, pp. 86-87, and Baum, pp. 290-292.

Baum, and others do link lines in the poem to objects and events in Poe's life. Starting with these realistic details, one can next move to the two women involved, Mrs. Stanard and Mrs. Allan. Poe in truth idealized them. Thus the most significant point is Poe's statement that Mrs. Stanard was "the first, purely ideal love of [his] soul." This idea would give one the clue to the movement in the poem from the literal face and figure of a woman to the idealization of that woman as a representative of spiritual love. The legend of Helen, then, becomes the symbol to express the reality in Poe's life. Although Helen is ultimately idealized in terms of spiritual love and although she may represent *woman* rather than a specific woman, one can find the basis of this pattern in Poe's own attitudes toward Mrs. Stanard and Mrs. Allan. Like many writers, Poe was using the power of his imagination, particularly its ability to create symbols in an artistic form, to universalize his particular feelings.

In the essay on "To Helen," the research was misdirected almost entirely toward pure biography and toward disagreements among critics of Poe. As soon as one channels the research data toward an interpretation of the poem, he will demonstrate the literary relevance of his efforts, and he will avoid the substitution of research for analysis.

EVALUATION OF CRITICISM

In recent years there has been a widespread emphasis upon literary criticism, particularly upon analysis of individual works and evaluation of the entire body of an author's work. Modern critics, frequently using newly developed areas of learning like psychology and anthropology, have often challenged traditional interpretations, and other scholars have published articles in rebuttal. Hence the evaluation of criticism on a given work or author could involve the student in considerable controversy.

Under such circumstances he could deliver merely an organized summation of the criticisms, because he might feel that the differences of opinion among the critics create so much confusion that he as an amateur cannot possibly straighten them out. If one simply classifies and summarizes the analyses, he may be bowing to a very common attitude among students. This attitude is frequently posed in a question, "Since so much has been said by the professionals, how can I add anything?" But this attitude may lead to a loss of the independent thinking which, as we have seen, is so vital to literary interpretation.

Although a beginner cannot be expected to deliver revolutionary pronouncements, he can at least take sides in a controversy on the basis of his own reading. He should evaluate the various interpretations as objectively and as logically as possible. He will probably discover that it is easier to express his disagreements than it is to support a position. On the other hand, he will at times find himself in such complete agreement with a critic that he feels the professional is saying in happier language what he himself might have said. In either case he should do more than repeat what the critic has said: he should try to find details and generalizations that will reinforce the interpretation he considers valid. By treating different points of view in this way, he will avoid summary and will use the opportunity to express himself. He must remember, however, that whether he is taking a position pro or con, his thesis must be substantiated by convincing evidence.

In such a research paper, one will on occasion have the opportunity to develop a compromise interpretation by adapting what he considers the best concepts in the various criticisms he is evaluating. In this way the student can make a worth-while synthesis of the material before him. This kind of research operates at its best when the student's examination of many criticisms stimulates him to derive a new approach to the work being discussed. Such an essay would combine both an evaluation of the research data and the development of a new interpretation.

In addition to such problems of content, the student will encounter difficulties with the organization of an essay involving a substantial number of criticisms. No one pattern of organization can be recommended because the material and the purposes of the student would vary so much. The main problem can be posed, however: should the criticisms be discussed one by one or according to carefully developed topics? If they are presented one by one, the writer—and also the reader—may have trouble linking ideas involved in the separate essays. As we have seen in the section on the organization of a comparison theme, the topical approach is very effective and allows one to make the necessary connections between the separate units being incorporated into the research paper. In dealing with a large body of material, however, a writer may find his problems immensely complicated if he uses the topical approach. In this case, the preparation before the writing of a first draft would have to be extremely intensive—particularly the note-taking and the arrangement of the cards.

To illustrate the use of printed criticism in a research paper, let us examine an essay, designedly uncomplicated and brief as research papers go, on a controversy about Shakespeare's Sonnet 73, the text of which appears on page 52.

Pessimism, Optimism, or Paradox?

A recent lively critical controversy about the interpretation of Shakespeare's Sonnet 73 has raised questions about the meaning and tone of the poem. Is it completely negative, emphasizing man's death, as some critics claim? Does it develop a positive tone, as James Schroeter, who attacks the traditional and negative view, insists? Or is it a tragic concept of man alleviated slightly by the awareness of the endurance of love, as Richard B. Hovey, who criticizes Schroeter's view, claims? Perhaps there is room for an interpretation resolving the differences between Schroeter and Hovey. In this resolution, the poem may represent a recognition of a paradox of human existence: from dying comes an intensification of one of man's most vital experiences—love.

Schroeter's essay precipitated the controversy.[1] He argues that the poem is not the "pessimistic utterance of a dying man," as previous critics have maintained. To support his contention, he distinguishes between what he calls primary and secondary images in the sonnet. The primary metaphors are "warm and positive"—autumn, twilight, and fire. These, according to Schroeter, can be related to the pleasantest of human experiences—for example, fall with its abundant harvest and radiant colorful display of leaves; twilight, which offers man a relief from labor; and firelight, which provides the atmosphere for friendship and good cheer.

The secondary images, on the other hand, connote "desolation, deprivation, or death"—the birds leaving their boughs, night obliterating the light of day, and fire reducing something to nothingness. Because these images are more active in the poem, the reader tends to focus on the desolation of winter, the blackness of night, and extinction by flame, rather than upon the warmth and cheer implicit in autumn, twilight, and fire. For this reason, Schroeter argues, scholars have concentrated on annihilation rather than on old age.

Schroeter maintains that actually the primary images bring out "a special kind of beauty, that 'aching sweetness' or nostalgia

1. James Schroeter, "Shakespeare's Not 'To-Be-Pitied Lover,'" *College English,* XXIII (January, 1962), 250-255.

so characteristic of Renaissance poetry." In the context of the secondary images, the primary ones blend pleasure and pain — pleasure from an awareness of beauty and pain from the recognition of the ephemeral nature of the experience.

As a result of this "aching sweetness," the last line is effective because it gives the reader "the sudden perception that all the images to which the narrator is compared are *primarily* pleasurable rather than painful, beautiful rather than ugly, and that their special quality of beauty is heightened rather than diminished by the pain."

In answer to this interpretation, Richard B. Hovey denies that images of autumn, twilight, and fire "are always, or even generally, cheerful and pleasant."[2] More important, he claims that the connotations of the primary images — for example, the abundance of fall and the beauty of a sunset — exist only in Schroeter's imagination.

Hovey insists that the three main images point "to universally natural and human phenomena — to an inevitable part of existence as we know it. We cannot escape the facts of transience, decay, and death." However, Shakespeare, Hovey claims, has made "our tragic awareness" a bit more bearable by hinting that love is enduring. Schroeter, according to Hovey, ignores "the heart of this sonnet: love."

This controversy really focuses attention on an aspect of the poem which neither Schroeter nor Hovey faces directly — the paradoxes of man's existence in the movements of time and in the cycles and phenomena of nature.

The text of the sonnet contains numerous paradoxes — the juxtaposition of the "bare ruined choirs" and the birds that once sang on the boughs of the trees (death and life); line thirteen which covers in one natural phenomenon, fire, both nourishment and consumption; the final couplet which combines aging and dying, a negative physical deterioration, with a growth of love, a strengthening of an inward feeling. The opposites contradicting and complementing one another give the poem its power and its meaning.

The paradoxes can also be seen in the cycles of imagery — that lightly stressed (autumn, twilight, fire), that strongly

2. Richard B. Hovey, "Sonnet 73," *College English,* XXIII (May, 1962), 672-673. Schroeter's "Reply" to Hovey is reprinted on p. 673 of the same issue; the answer substantially repeats Schroeter's arguments. In the same issue there is another controversy, this time between Schroeter and Robert Berkelman, one of the earlier interpreters taking the pessimistic view. This argument pertains to whether time passes in the poem. See *College English,* XXIII (May, 1962), 674-675.

stressed (winter, night, ashes) and that implied if the cycle continues (spring, morning, and the Phoenix, which according to legend rises out of the ashes to be reborn). The implied imagery connotes in each case a rebirth. When these are related to the human condition, the growth of love in a sense parallels spring, morning, and the Phoenix.

However, the poem is not as triumphant as the implication of rebirth might indicate. Like all paradoxes, the basic one in the poem is of mixed tone. The tone consists of Shakespeare's tragic awareness of the ever-continuing and coinciding cycles of experience—the negative and positive states in nature and in man. More important, the sonnet makes the negative and the positive simultaneous. Just as in final triumph Hamlet dies, so for the narrator of the sonnet there is in dying a new intensification of love.

Therefore, Hovey's insistence that the poem is about love is probably right, just as Schroeter's fight against a completely negative view is justified. Hovey perhaps sees too little of the positive tone in the emphasis on love; Schroeter perhaps emphasizes too much the positive elements of the primary imagery. Neither stresses the implied imagery which helps create the effective paradoxes of the sonnet.

In this essay, the research is minimal, confined to two issues of *College English*, and there is no attempt to review all or much of the commentary on the sonnet. Despite this limitation, the paper does focus on important issues stirred up by the two critics. The essay summarizes much of what they say. If summary were the only contribution of the paper, then it would not be very significant. The essay's chief virtue lies in the attempt to use the controversial views to point up a new way to approach the sonnet. In other words, the writer is not performing the function of a parrot; he is expressing independent thought based on the limited research.

RESEARCH
AND THE CREATIVE PROCESS

When confronted with several interpretations of a literary work, students will frequently ask, "What did the author intend?" It is difficult to offer an answer to this question for all literary works. However, in many cases one can combine his intrinsic analysis of the purpose of a work with research into the creative process of the author.

Even when a great deal of insight into the creative process is available, one has to realize that an author is not always aware of everything he puts into his story or poem. Although an over-emphasis on the unconscious intentions of an author can lead to excessive in-reading, one must be aware of them, especially if the text of the work supports one's interpretation.

There are basically three ways to do research on an author's creative process in a poem or story: (1) examine his sources, the material which he used but reshaped into his own imaginative creation; (2) study his stated intentions or the private development of a work in notebooks, journals, letters, and drafts; and (3) analyze any changes made by the author if the work was revised or reprinted. Although these paths can become highly specialized, for some authors and works they could yield a rewarding experience to the student.

To compare the source of Shakespeare's *Othello* with the play is such an experience. A careful comparison would provide a great deal of information about how Shakespeare transformed a crude melodramatic story by Cinthio into a well-disciplined tragedy. One would have a unique opportunity to look into the playwright's workshop and to examine the technical resources he employed. If one were writing a paper on his investigation of a source, he would have to remember that he is concerned with the analysis of meaning and technique and not merely with proving that the author used the source.

Although we have no journals or notebooks of Shakespeare, we do have statements by some authors of their intentions, as well as private notes and trial runs relevant to the works. In studying the stories or novels of Henry James, one would be unwise indeed to ignore his notebooks and the "Prefaces" which he wrote for the New York edition of his works. One could, for instance, actually determine how James resolved some of the technical problems he encountered. This kind of study allows one to understand how an author operates and precisely what he is trying to accomplish in a particular work.

In some cases the changes an author made in the text of his work can provide insight into meaning and technique. The first version of "To Helen" is inferior to the second, whereas the final text of "La Belle Dame" is not nearly as good as the first one, which Keats wrote in a letter to his brother. Why did Poe and Keats make these changes? Do the alterations provide information about their intentions and thus help one comprehend meanings and artistry? These are questions which research can help answer.

If the student ignores the author's intention as he has stated it or as it can be inferred from an analysis of the work itself, he can produce unsound interpretation. An example of this fallacy is an interpretation of "Flowering Judas" by Ray B. West, Jr. West attributes to Braggioni the possibility of redemption. On the other hand, he sees Laura as emotionally dead, incapable of any kind of love.[1] The story itself can be used to refute this view. The intrinsic intention of the story is reasonably clear because throughout the narrative Miss Porter heaps sarcasm and irony upon Braggioni. In addition, Braggioni's attitude toward Eugenio, when compared with the guilt-ridden sympathy of Laura, indicates that in the context of revolution Braggioni, not Laura, is emotionally dead. To some readers he emerges as the Judas of the story.

Such an interpretation of the intrinsic intent of the story can be corroborated by Miss Porter's own account of how it was written. This has been made public in *This Is My Best*, an anthology edited by Whit Burnett, and in a talk delivered by Miss Porter at the University of Wichita on September 27, 1961. The statement in *This Is My Best* demonstrates the author's sympathy with the plight of Laura, with "the desperate complications of her mind and feelings" and with her "self-delusion," the central idea of the story.[2] In her talk Miss Porter stated that when she was in Mexico — the life experience behind the story — she became acquainted with two kinds of revolutionists: those who died for what they believed and those who "were frauds, criminals, careerists, hangers-on, exploiters." "Flowering Judas," she said, was written about one of the frauds, Braggioni, the fictional representation of a real person. Throughout her discussion her sympathetic attitude toward Laura, whose characterization was based on a friend, contrasted sharply with her hostility toward Braggioni. These contrasting attitudes would help one establish the author's intention and tone and would probably cause him to reject West's interpretation, which seems to reverse Miss Porter's own concept of her purpose.

As an example of a study employing research to examine an author's shaping of his purpose and the materials available

1. Ray B. West, Jr., "Katherine Anne Porter: Symbol and Theme in 'Flowering Judas,'" *Accent*, VII (Spring, 1947), 182-188.
2. Katherine Anne Porter, "Why She Selected 'Flowering Judas,'" *This Is My Best*, ed. Whit Burnett (New York, 1942), pp. 539-540.

to him, examine the following essay on Nathaniel Hawthorne's story "The Ambitious Guest." The research is unobtrusive and serves several useful functions: to establish Hawthorne's knowledge of the facts of the slide, to present one account of the actual events, and to refer to some other interpretations of the story. However, the main purpose of the essay is to show how Hawthorne transformed an actual happening into a carefully constructed story. Interpretation is most prominent in the essay, but without the research the analysis would not be so effective.

"The Ambitious Guest": From Fact to Fiction*

Hawthorne scholars have long known that "The Ambitious Guest" (1835) was based on a landslide which occurred in August, 1826, in the White Mountains of New Hampshire. That Hawthorne knew the details of the disaster is certain. He must have heard of the landslide during his trips to the White Mountains;[1] he may even have learned of it earlier from the Salem newspapers.[2] Because of his close relationship with Samuel Goodrich, Hawthorne was probably acquainted with the facts as they are presented with reasonable accuracy in Peter Parley books.[3]

More important than his knowledge of the facts is what Hawthorne's imagination did to them. By relating the event to the story, we can acquire a glimpse into the creative workshop of a literary artist who shapes meaning by technique.

Although the single source of Hawthorne's knowledge cannot be and need not be determined, one can find a substantial account of the catastrophe in Goodrich's *A System of Universal Geography* (1832):

> The Notch of the White Mountains will long be remembered for the tragical fate of a whole family, who were swept away by a *slide*, or avalanche of earth from the side of the mountain, on the night of the 28th of August, 1826. This

---

*This article appeared originally in the October 1952 issue of the *Boston Public Library Quarterly* and is reprinted here, revised by the author, with permission.
1. Elizabeth Chandler, "A Study of the Sources of the Tales and Romances Written by Hawthorne before 1853," *Smith College Studies in Modern Languages*, VII, No. 4 (July, 1926), 4, 16.
2. See *Essex Register*, September 7, 1826, and *Salem Literary Observer*, September 9, 1826.
3. See the following Parley books edited by Goodrich: *A System of Universal Geography* (Cincinnati, 1832), p. 27; *The Child's Book of American Geography* (Boston, 1831), p. 15; *The First Book of History for Children and Youth* (Cincinnati, 1831), p. 14; and *Peter Parley's Book of Curiosities* (New York, 1831), pp. 141-142. For numerous other accounts of the slide and for a useful interpretation of the story, see Kenneth Walter Cameron, *Genesis of Hawthorne's "The Ambitious Guest"* (Hartford, Conn., 1955).

family by the name of Willey, occupied what was called the Notch House, in a very narrow interval between the bases of the two mountains. No knowledge of any incident from the mountains in former times existed to create any apprehension of danger in their situation. Their dwelling stood alone, many miles from the residence of any human being, and there was an aspect of rural neatness, simplicity and content in their manner of life, that strongly interested the traveller whom chance and curiosity led into their neighborhood. For two seasons previous, the mountains had been very dry, and on the 28th of June there was a slide not far from the house, which so far alarmed them, that they erected a temporary encampment a short distance from their dwelling, as a place of refuge.

On the morning of August 28th it began raining very hard with a strong and tempestuous wind. The storm continued through the day and night, but it appears the family retired to rest without the least apprehension of any disaster. Among them were five beautiful children, from two to twelve years of age. At midnight the clouds which had gathered about the mountain, seemed to burst instantaneously, and pour their contents down in one tremendous flood of rain. . . . The avalanche began upon the mountain top above the house, and moved down the mountain in a direct line toward it, in a sweeping torrent which seemed like a river pouring from the clouds, full of trees, earth and rocks.

On reaching the house it divided in a singular manner within six feet of it, passed on either side, sweeping away the stable and horses, and completely surrounding the dwelling. . . . The family, it appears, sprang from their beds, and fled naked into the open air, where they were instantly carried away by the torrents and overwhelmed . . . .

In the morning, a most frightful scene of desolation was exhibited . . . .

The barn was crushed . . . but the house was uninjured. The beds appeared to have been just quitted. . . . The bodies of seven of the family were dug out of the drift wood and mountain ruins, on the banks of the Saco.

In accordance with these facts, Hawthorne indicates the solitude of the family in his story and describes their simple contentment; and it was probably the mention of a "traveller" that suggested to him the guest. The "temporary encampment"

of the account becomes the "barrier" which had been reared for
an emergency. He speaks of the wind that "came through the
Notch," of the slide which "broke into two branches," and finally
of the valley of the Saco.[4]

However, Hawthorne made many changes in the account
to suit the artistic mold of his story — the folly of excessive
ambition and desire for earthly immortality. For example, he
does not have the family sleeping when the slide occurs, for he
needs them awake to greet the guest and to serve as his audience.
In his version, the bodies of the victims are not discovered
because he wishes the guest to remain unknown, his ambitions
for fame and immortality a grim irony lost in the debris.

But it is in the account of the people killed that the most
interesting changes occur. Hawthorne introduces a daughter of
seventeen, "the image of Happiness," to whom the guest is immediately attracted, and also an aged grandmother, "the image
of Happiness grown old." These additions to the members of
the family of the original version (mother, father, and young
children) give the strange guest an audience which represents
every important age of man, in effect a symbol of mankind
itself: extreme youth, ebullient and innocent; blushing, healthy
adolescence; calm and earnest maturity; and superstitious age.

Although Hawthorne was aware that guests visited the
family of real life, the guest in the story is his own creation.
In fact, through the stranger Hawthorne achieves the fusion
of theme and form.

Although the guest has been among the proud and haughty,
he is unlike other aristocrats in Hawthorne's fiction such as Lady
Eleanore and Lord de Vere. He does not hesitate "to stoop his
head to the lowly cottage door, and be like a brother or a son at the
poor man's fireside." Yet these wholesome impulses and the "prophetic sympathy" he feels for the family are counterbalanced
by the driving motivation of his life, "a high and abstracted
ambition" to be known by posterity. In the characterization of
the guest, therefore, Hawthorne achieves a double purpose:
to make the reader sympathize with him because of his warm
rapport with the family and yet to stir up the fearful premonition
implicit in the man's monomania.

Having created the guest, Hawthorne builds around him
both the theme and structure of his story.[5] During the course

4. All references to "The Ambitious Guest" are in George Parsons Lathrop, ed., *The Complete
Works of Nathaniel Hawthorne,* Riverside Edition (Boston, 1882), I, 364-374.
5. For a dissenting interpretation which stresses the family rather than the guest, see C.
Hobart Edgren, "Hawthorne's 'The Ambitious Guest': An Interpretation," *Nineteenth-Century
Fiction,* X (September, 1955), 151-156.

of the frank conversation that develops between the guest and the family, each person, representative as he is of a stage in man's growth, expresses an ambition. Thus the structure consists of a series of modest wishes on the part of the humble family which contrast ironically with the lofty aspirations of the guest.

The guest's ambition is reflected in his passionate statement: "I cannot die till I have achieved my destiny. Then, let Death come! I shall have built my monument!" It is apparent that he envisions a lofty destiny, whereas the others seek a humble lot. In ironic contrast to his wish (with its premonition of death) is the adolescent girl's desire to have the plain comfort of home life. She desires no fame; she speaks not of death but of simple life.

The father's ambition also contrasts sharply with that of the stranger, though it is more associated with life outside the house than is the daughter's wish. "I should want," he says, "to stand well with my neighbors and be called Squire, and sent to General Court for a term or two. . . ." When he dies (another striking upon the note of death), he hopes for a simple gravestone with something on it to let people know that he lived "an honest man and died a Christian." The monument he desires lacks the enormity of the one which the guest seeks.

The most trivial of the wishes comes from one of the children, who are "outvying each other in wild wishes, and childish projects of what they would do when they [come] to be men and women." He clamors that all of them should go to take a drink out of the basin of the Flume. The wish is almost translated into concrete fulfillment when a wagon which could have taken them to the Flume, and perhaps to safety, stops momentarily at their door. But the wish for life-giving water merely stirs up laughter. Ironically death ensues because this trivial wish is ignored.

The death to come is also reflected in the grandmother's simple yet weird desire based on a superstition. Troubled by the fear that if anything in the attire of a corpse were amiss it would attempt to mend the error, she requests one of the children to hold a looking-glass over her face when she lies in her coffin, so that she can see if everything is arranged correctly.

Although he has used previous wishes of the others as a point of departure to reinforce his own desire for an immortal monument on earth, the guest seizes upon this climactic wish of the old woman to project his monomania again and yet to reveal the impending anonymity of his own death. He says, "Old and young, we dream of graves and monuments. . . . I wonder how mariners feel when the ship is sinking, and they, unknown and undistinguished, are to be buried together in the ocean — that wide and nameless sepulchre?" This remark introduces the final irony of the story — an irony that relates to both meaning and structure — the manner of their death. If they had remained inside, they would have been spared, for the slide divided immediately above the house and left it untouched. The stranger now has his nameless sepulchre. The grandmother's vanity remains unsatisfied; the father will have neither his title of Squire nor his simple gravestone; the young girl will have no husband or comfortable fireside; the child will never drink from the Flume.

Using all the other ambitions merely to emphasize the zealous aspiration of the stranger, Hawthorne is ready to sum up his moral:

> Woe for the high-souled youth, with his dream of Earthly Immortality! His name and person utterly unknown; his history, his way of life, his plans, a mystery never to be solved, his death and his existence equally a doubt! Whose was the agony of that death moment?

Although this moral is perhaps too direct and unartistic, it has at least been prepared for artistically by Hawthorne's emphasis upon death, by his use of irony, but, most important, by his skillful fusion of theme and structure. Other artistic devices used by Hawthorne also point to the theme of the story and lift it beyond a factual account of a family tragedy.

The premonition of death so important to the structure of the story and to the ironic contrast between the guest's ambition and his real fate is considerably amplified by a rhythmical motif in descriptions of the setting. The very first sentence of the story mentions "ruins of great trees which had come crashing down the precipice." The setting of the house is "a dangerous one," at the foot of mountains which often send stones rumbling down the valley. The wailing wind also prefigures trouble as the guest enters the house. Just as he draws a chair near the fire, all hear the rumbling of rocks. This leads the father to refer to the safety of the nearby shelter — a note of irony which is made apparent by the noises of the wind growing louder and drearier. The setting in the house is bright and warm, but it cannot dissipate the motif of doom stirring outside.

Hawthorne's "remarkable use of line," the movement up and

down and transverse, has been discussed in some detail.[6] The upward movement of line is even represented in the guest's haughty mien; at the same time, he does not hesitate to stoop (downward movement) to enter a humble household. Of course, the most important line is downward, for it signifies the direction of the slide which is to destroy everyone, and at the same time the futility of ambition. The splitting of the slide also creates an image of line movement which surrounds but misses the house — an association of a fine art device with the quirks of destiny.

All of these artistic touches reinforce Hawthorne's use of ironic contrast, his emphasis upon premonition, and his carefully worked-out structure. Thus a drab set of facts has been imaginatively lifted to an artistic expression of an enduring truth about man's prideful ambition.

6. See Leland Schubert, *Hawthorne, the Artist: Fine Art Devices in Fiction* (Chapel Hill, 1944), pp. 47-49.

GLOSSARY

Allegory is a form of narrative in which everything in the surface plot stands for something else. That is, a reader can make exact symbolical equations relating characters, places, or actions to the meanings for which they stand. Since abstract moral qualities and emotions are frequently given human form (see *Personification*), the characters in an allegory are often flat and unreal, types rather than individuals. A good example of pure allegory is Bunyan's *Pilgrim's Progress,* a story about the journey of Christian (Christian man) toward salvation, a journey full of allegorical impediments. In some cases, such as Swift's *Gulliver's Travels* and Dante's *Divine Comedy,* the allegory operates at more than one level simultaneously. For instance, in Swift's story the surface plot at times has two concurrent strands of meaning and satire directed at political events and at human nature.

When a narrative is highly symbolical, one has to decide whether it is an allegory. If the work deals realistically with human beings, if it does not use personification persistently or at all, and if the symbolism is so complex and suggestive that direct equations cannot be made, it is probably not an allegory. For example, although the events in *Huckleberry Finn* can be frequently interpreted in terms of man as a moral or immoral being, the story is so real and so human that it would not be considered an allegory. Yet there are symbolic narratives which are bizarre, unnatural, or supernatural (some stories by Hawthorne and Kafka or Coleridge's "The Ancient Mariner"). In these the symbolism is so complex and suggestive that it is impossible to reduce them to the direct personifications and abstractions of *Pilgrim's Progress*. In allegories, except such intricate works as those of Swift and Dante, there is far less opportunity for multiple interpretation than there would be in difficult symbolical narratives, based either on real life or on the unusual or the supernatural.

Alliteration, a technique which enhances verbal music, is generally considered the repetition of initial sounds of words, usually consonants. In Poe's "To Helen" are lines like "The *w*eary, *w*ay-*w*orn *w*anderer bore" and "To the *g*lory that was *G*reece, / And the *g*randeur that was Rome." In Macbeth's speech responding to the news of his wife's death are alliterative phrases like "*p*etty *p*ace," "*d*ay to *d*ay," "*d*usty *d*eath," and "*p*oor *p*layer." Although the words which create alliteration may have been chosen by Shakespeare and Poe for their sound effects, we should note that they are extremely appropriate to the meanings conveyed by the poetry.

Allusion is a reference, real or fictional, to someone, some event, or something in the Bible, literature, history, or any aspect of culture. The reference naturally preserves its original meaning but must be put into the context of the work being analyzed. Only by this procedure can one determine whether the author is incorporating the allusion directly, altering or modifying it, or reversing it ironically. (See pp. 5-7; see also *Myth*.)

Ambiguity is a term used to describe words, figures of speech, and also actions in literary works for which more than one meaning is possible. Ambiguity may be due to the subtlety of an author's art, or it may stem from his confusion. It is undesirable if it does not enrich the literary work or if it causes confusion. Ambiguity is the source of multiple interpretation: that is, different people can interpret the same words and events in opposite ways because of the suggestive power of the poem or story. For example, is the title "La Belle Dame sans Merci" to be taken literally as an indictment of the supernatural lady, or is it a reflection of the lack of faith in the pursuit of beauty? One should also note the controversy about Shakespeare's Sonnet 73; perhaps this is due to the heavy emphasis on paradox, which is a kind of ambiguity finally resolved into a sensible coupling of opposites. In "Flowering Judas," Miss Porter, an omniscient author, deliberately leaves the fate of Laura unresolved. In "Old Mr. Marblehall," the second life of the central character is vividly yet ambiguously portrayed. To determine whether it is reality or fantasy, one has to examine the evidence of language and details very carefully. Even in a story as unambiguous as "The Ambitious Guest," there has been debate about whether Hawthorne's final question "Whose was the agony of that death moment?" applies to the guest or to the family. Ambiguity, therefore, is relevant to many important aspects of literary analysis: an author's style, his choice of words and his use of figures of speech, especially symbols; the motivations of characters; the implications of settings, situations, and endings.

Assonance refers to the repetition of internal vowel sounds. Particularly in oral presentation, such sounds contribute to the musical quality of poetry (for example, the *e, a,* and *o* sounds in "To Helen"). At the same time, assonance can suggest the moods and meanings of poetry. In the sonnet "On First Looking into Chapman's Homer," the expansiveness of the vowel sounds adds to the vast dimensions of discovery described in the poem. Assonance is prominent in the following description of setting which creates atmosphere in "The Rime of the Ancient Mariner":

> The ice was here, the ice was there,
> The ice was all around:
> It cracked and growled, and roared and howled,
> Like noises in a swound!

Atmosphere signifies the mood or moods of a literary work created by the description of settings, by the actions and words of characters, by the tone of an author or the voice through which he speaks. Atmosphere is related to suspense in that it can create tenseness and expectations within a reader or observer. It is also pertinent to a study of structure in that a consistent atmosphere (as in Poe's "The Fall of the House of Usher") helps to unify a story, poem, or play. In longer works such as *Huckleberry Finn*, the atmosphere can shift as the situations and settings alter. In drama performed on the stage, the physical manifestations of a setting (suggested by stage directions and/or dialog) are important to the atmosphere which the playwright wants to establish. Eugene O'Neill stresses the hovering elm tree in *Desire under the Elms* and the persistent fog in *Anna Christie* and in *Bound East for Cardiff.*

"The Ambitious Guest" offers an interesting contrast of atmospheres through the description of two simultaneous settings: inside the house there is the cheer and warmth of the family and the fireside; outside there are the fearful, premonitory sounds of wind and falling rocks. Even inside the house an atmosphere of doom is created by the constant emphasis upon death. In "Old Mr. Marblehall," there are the conflicting atmospheres of the cold indifference among the townsmen and of the vivid fantasy within Marblehall. Even the settings of the old man's two existences — the family mansion and the submerged and dusty suburban dwelling — radiate different atmospheres.

Ballad is a narrative song. Popular ballads have been handed down by oral tradition; hence, there can be numerous versions of the same ballad, and no one individual can be credited as the author of a folk ballad. A ballad generally contains a simple but dramatic narrative for which little background is provided. The story and emotional force of the ballad are usually conveyed by dialog; understatement of the situation and repetition (refrain) contribute to the power of ballads. Examples of traditional folk ballads are "Sir Patrick Spens," "Edward," and "Barbara Allan."

A literary ballad is an imitation of a folk or popular ballad. "La Belle Dame sans Merci" is considered a literary ballad, as is the much longer narrative poem, Coleridge's "The Rime of the Ancient Mariner."

Blank Verse is unrhymed iambic pentameter. It is frequently used in poetry and also in poetic drama, perhaps because it is more natural and closer to speech than most metrical lines. Despite the regularity of the meter, blank verse is open to subtle variations by means of a shift in the pauses within lines, or of run-on lines, or of slight alterations of the iambic pattern. Blank verse is also amazingly flexible in range: it can be used for grand and dignified, meditative, dramatic, emotional, or conversational poetry. To discover this flexibility, compare passages from Milton's *Paradise Lost*, from Shakespeare's plays, and from Frost's "Birches."

Caesura is the main internal pause of a line of poetry. The pause can be dictated by punctuation, grammar, natural stops in speech, or rhetorical emphasis in oral delivery. The mark designating a caesura (//) does not indicate the duration of the pause. Even if the placement of caesuras can be agreed upon, the length of the pause may vary with the individual reader.

Pauses contribute to the rhythm of poetry. When they are varied, they help a poet avoid the monotony of regular meters, especially in closed couplets (two rhymed self-contained lines). A line of poetry which requires a pause at its end is said to be end-stopped.

In the following group of couplets from "An Essay on Criticism," Pope varies the caesura by placing it after the fourth and fifth syllables. In one line he establishes two equal pauses:

First follow nature, // and your judgment frame
By her just standard, // which is still the same:
Unerring nature, // still divinely bright,
One clear, unchanged, // and universal light,
Life, force, and beauty, // must to all impart,
At once the source, // and end, // and test of art.

In "La Belle Dame sans Merci" there is a dramatic use of a double caesura to stress the barrenness of the natural setting:

And no // birds // sing.

Caricature is an unsubtle, oversimplified, and exaggerated presentation of a character, generally stressing only one aspect, so that the reader understands what the character represents. Since caricature is sometimes designed to make a person or a type of person seem ridiculous, it is a kind of satire. Frequently stressing physical description, caricature represents in words what an artist attempts to do in cartoons. Some examples of portraits in caricature are Osric, the effeminate dandy in *Hamlet*; Ichabod Crane, the Yankee schoolmaster in Irving's "The Legend of Sleepy Hollow"; and Scrooge, the harsh penny pincher in Dickens' *A Christmas Carol*.

Characterization is the means whereby an author establishes the illusion that the persons created by his words are indeed people or like people, with traits and personalities which a reader can recognize and analyze. These characters may be developed by means of one technique or a combination of techniques:

1) Physical description
2) Depiction of the character's actions and words
3) Portrayal of the character's innermost dreams, feelings, and thoughts; of the character's internal struggle and agonies or his groping toward consciousness — that is, toward awareness or understanding of himself and his context

4) Clarification of the character's motives, the reasons for his actions or the forces which make him perform as he does

5) Establishment of adequate reasons for any change in the character within the span of the story

6) Emphasis upon conflicts—for example, a character's responses to other people or to his environment (see *Conflict*)

7) Emphasis upon what other characters say about the person being analyzed

8) Use of contrast—that is, allowing the reader to compare the character with someone else in the story

9) The author's direct comments, analysis, or tone

Analysis of characters is fundamental to the reading of most fiction. In drama, since the author provides the words and actions which the actors convey, characterization is extremely important and of course is enhanced by the added dimension of live performance. In narrative poems, characterization can be vital. In dramatic monologs, a kind of poetry in which one person speaks usually to someone who does not respond in dialog, the speaker reveals his own character (for example, the Duke in Browning's "My Last Duchess" and Prufrock in Eliot's "Love Song of J. Alfred Prufrock").

Characterization is related to other technical aspects. The actions and words of characters constitute much of the plot of a narrative and hence must be considered in analyzing plot structure. Point of view is also relevant; for example, the omnisciency of the author or the revelations of a narrator can help one analyze a character. An author's style—for instance, his descriptive powers or his tone—can also assist in portraying a character.

Laura, in "Flowering Judas," is a good example of characterization, for, in creating her, Miss Porter uses many of the means listed above. For example, by description, Miss Porter effectively establishes the physical attractiveness of Laura despite the fact that she wears thick and heavy clothing. Her physical ripeness is important in terms of her restraint and her negative attitude toward those who have courted her and toward Braggioni's unsubtle sexual desire. In addition to outward description, Miss Porter provides glimpses into Laura's mind and emotions: her fear of "a shocking death"; her self-condemnation; and, most important, her guilty conscience revealed in her dream. In addition, Miss Porter contrasts Laura with Braggioni throughout the story—his unattractive bulk and her attractiveness or his attitude toward Eugenio compared with hers. Miss Porter also provides direct commentary about Laura: her statement that Laura "is not at home in the world." By detecting and analyzing these and other means which Miss Porter employs to create her character, one can make a worth-while analysis of Laura's character and her significance to the story's meaning.

Whereas Laura is developed largely by the technique of an omniscient author, the barber in "Haircut" reveals his own character through his dramatic monolog. In displaying himself he also unconsciously underscores the malice of Jim, whose exploits seem so appealing to him. Although the barber's speech is full of grammatical and syntactical errors, this characteristic alone could not account for his limited mentality. The limitations of his mind are seen most clearly in his literal-mindedness and in his response to Jim. His explanation of Jim's obvious pun about being canned from a canning factory, his repetition of the condoning statement that Jim is a card, and his failure to see that Jim was murdered by the half-wit Paul (an effective irony) mark the barber as basically stupid. This chief characteristic he himself reveals.

Climax in narrative works — prose fiction, poetry, or drama — is the highest or most important point toward which the chain of events has been moving. It can be the point at which issues and conflicts in the plot are fully and clearly resolved, or it can establish the circumstances which allow the author to explain and unravel the events (see *Denouement*). A climax can also be ironic, involving a reversal or backfiring of events, or it can be ambiguous, leaving the reader to contemplate the implications of what the author does not tell him. (See pp. 20-21.)

In "Old Mr. Marblehall," there is no specific climax because there is little or no plot. Most of the story is the author's ordered speculation about Marblehall, who is taking his walk. The climax would be Marblehall's shocking the town. Yet this climax exists only in the projection by the point of view into the second son's possible discovery and into the wishful thinking of Marblehall. Since the second life probably does not exist, there can be no real climax in the story except the reader's final recognition of Marblehall's failure.

Comedy is generally considered a type of drama constructed to entertain, induce laughter, and at times provide searching commentary on human nature and society. The range of comedy, running the gamut from farce (broadly exaggerated fun such as slapstick) to witty and highly sophisticated commentaries on life, is much more diverse than that of tragedy.

The tone of comedy also varies considerably. Some comedies are almost entirely light and frothy, while others, through the laughter and thought invoked by tools like satire, are serious analyses of human foibles and vices. During the seventeenth and eighteenth centuries, comedy was often used to expose fashionable customs such as gambling or dueling and also to condemn such human weaknesses or sins as superstition, gullibility, vanity, extravagance, hypocrisy, and greed.

Although comedy can deal with serious issues, it is generally far less tense than tragedy. For example, although it is possible to view the characterization of Shylock in *The Merchant of Venice* seriously, that play is not nearly as tense as *Othello* or *King Lear* and, in fact, concludes with a very light last act.

The characters in a comedy are usually not complex or well-rounded. If they are too fully developed, the play would probably become serious drama. In some comedies the playwright uses a character or characters as a kind of social norm against which others in the play are measured. In Congreve's *The Way of the World* (1700), the hero and heroine, Mirabell and Millamant, serve as models of good taste and good behavior. In such cases the protagonists (the characters obviously favored by the author) can be more fully presented. In many comedies, however, flat (one-dimensional) and stock (conventional or stereotyped) characters are represented.

Although the plot elements of a comedy can be unified, one does not apply the same standards of analysis that he might use for tragedy. The plot of a comedy tends to be episodic or extremely involved. Since the characters are not usually complicated, the emphasis in comedy is upon situations and actions which evoke laughter. These are frequently artificial or exaggerated. In the comedies of Shakespeare and of his contemporaries, disguise and cases of mistaken identity are frequent. A more modern example occurs in Goldsmith's *She Stoops to Conquer* when the hero mistakes a young lady of good family for the barmaid of a country inn.

This play, *She Stoops to Conquer*, reflects a basic ingredient of comic plot — incongruity, or the linking of inharmonious or opposite parts that create laughter. The discrepancy between what the hero thinks Kate Hardcastle is and what she really is provides comic amusement for the audience which is aware, all along, of the true situation. Similar involvements in comedies also emphasize the ludicrous — the absurd or the ridiculous. A fine example of such emphasis occurs in *Twelfth Night,* when

Malvolio, forgetting his age and station, appears fantastically dressed so that he may win the favors of Olivia.

The outcome of the events of a comic plot frequently involves the happy ending in which everything is neatly resolved (for example, the general reconciliation at the conclusion of *The Tempest*). At times, however, the butt of comic criticism gets his deserved punishment. Since he is not likely to attract the sympathy of an audience, his comeuppance usually proves comic rather than tragic (Malvolio in *Twelfth Night*).

Some comedies rely heavily on dialog to evoke laughter and thought. In such plays the dialog is usually witty, urbane, and sophisticated, and the brilliance of speeches can become more important than characterization or plot development. Oscar Wilde's delightful comedy, *The Importance of Being Earnest*, is an example of a play which has become a perennial favorite because of witty dialog. In such cases, one analyzes the playwright's style rather than his substance.

The impact of comedy on an audience has a vast range from the belly laugh to intellectual laughter. Although a person viewing a comedy can come away with insight into human nature, he is not likely to undergo catharsis (see *Tragedy*) or to feel a painful sense of waste as he might after witnessing a tragedy.

A student should not assume that the study of comedy is confined to drama, for in many stories and novels and in some poems one can discover comic elements—for instance, Irving's "The Legend of Sleepy Hollow," Fielding's *Joseph Andrews* and *Tom Jones*, Twain's *Huckleberry Finn*, Pope's "The Rape of the Lock," and Burns' "Tam O'Shanter."

Complication or Rising Action in stories denotes the development of actions and conflicts. In a traditional plot, the complication falls between the exposition and climax and is closely related to both. (See pp. 20-21.)

Even in a loosely constructed novel like *Huckleberry Finn*, a reader can determine complication in Huck's relationship with Jim. The escape of both from their environments—the expository element—brings them together in a series of experiences, and the complication involves their attitudes toward one another resulting from their own actions and those of others. Huck, for example, has to decide whether Jim is to be treated as a human being or as a slave. The complication includes his struggles within himself over this problem. When Huck instinctively defies conventions of society and determines not to surrender Jim, the complication is resolved and the climax occurs.

Conflict refers to the collision of opposing forces in narrative, drama, or poetry. Conflicts can take many forms:

1) Between people — as the husband and wife in "Birthday Party"

2) Between man and his environment (family, occupational circumstances, social and economic conditions beyond one's control, natural forces) — for example, the slide in "The Ambitious Guest" is a natural force conflicting with and annihilating the warmth of the family group and the lofty aspiration of the stranger; in "Old Mr. Marblehall," the old gentleman's sense of conflict with the town's attitude toward him is the only intense emotion in his colorless, correct existence

3) Between ideologies and concepts — as Laura's original idealistic acceptance of the revolution versus Braggioni's cynical exploitation of it; or the cynicism of the real world versus the Knight's visionary pursuit of an ideal beauty

4) Internal conflicts which can come from any of the forces above, from feelings entirely within a person, or from causes unknown — for instance, "The Heavy Bear" emphasizes a conflict between one's urges and instincts and his awareness of the need for restraint

Connotation and Denotation *Denotation* is the exact or dictionary meaning of a word as far as one can determine it. *Connotation,* on the other hand, involves the implications, inferences, or suggestive power of words, phrases, or figures of speech. (See pp. 1-3.)

Consonance is the repetition of internal and/or terminal consonant sounds. Sometimes an initial consonant can become part of a pattern of consonance. Usually the vowel sound before the repeated consonant changes and thus can establish important contrasts of sound and mood (for example, the words *cold* and *lull* used in "La Belle Dame"). In other words, the context of consonantal sounds must be considered.

An unsubtle demonstration of consonance occurs in the following made-up verse:

At the hall on the hill he stood
A lone and lean old man,
Weathered of sin and sun.

"La Belle Dame," however, illustrates an amazingly subtle display of consonance which merges music with moods, emotions, and ideas. The best example is the persistent recurrence of the *l* sound from the title to the next to the last line. In the Knight's account of his pursuit of the Lady, the *l* sound in context is usually pleasant and musical and hence contributes to the beauty of the visionary pursuit; note words like *beautiful, child, light, love, long, wild,* and *lulled.* On the other hand, the *l* sound in the context of the real world occasionally takes on an appropriately chilling or harsher sound, especially in the key phrases *cold hill's side* and *cold hill side.*

Context designates the surroundings in which an element of a literary work appears. (See pp. 5-7; 49-52.)

Convention in literary works denotes traditional practices, involving both technique and content, which accumulate as a literary type develops. In literary analysis a knowledge of conventions can help one recognize how an author develops meaning within a given work. It also allows one to determine whether an author is deviating from the traditions. In short, one's knowledge of conventions should be put in the context of the specific work being studied.

For example, the sonnet traditionally consists of fourteen lines (although some poems labeled sonnets are longer). Within the sonnet tradition, there are different types, each with its own conventions of rhyme and structure. In some Italian or Petrarchan sonnets, the poet uses eight lines (the octave) to present a question or to pose one point of view. The remaining six lines (the sestet) answer the question or offer an alternate or rebuttal to the first attitude. Milton's sonnet on his blindness is an excellent example of this convention: its octave indicates questioning and rebelliousness about his sightless state, but its sestet offers a resolution and reconciliation. Keats' sonnet on Chapman's Homer also follows the two-part division of the Italian sonnet; however, the sestet is essentially an elaboration of the octave rather than a response to it.

On the other hand, Sonnet 73 by Shakespeare follows the traditions established by the Elizabethan or Shakespearean sonnet. It consists of three four-line units (quatrains) and a concluding two lines (couplet), which sometimes seems to reverse the rest of the poem or to provide a surprise ending. This convention of structure obviously affects the content of Sonnet 73. Each of the three quatrains consists of a basic metaphor related to aging and dying. By introducing the intensification of love in the midst of dying, the couplet provides a surprising and paradoxical conclusion to the sonnet. In all of the examples cited, there is meaningful unity of the traditional parts—a fusing of structure and meaning.

Convention in regard to content may also enter into characterization and plot situations. In old-fashioned melodrama one finds the conventional villain who pursues and torments the heroine. In many plays plot incidents involving characters in disguise or people eavesdropping have become conventional.

Literary works contain numerous other conventions. For example, see *Elegy* and *Epic.*

Denouement is that portion of narrative plot which ties up the loose strands stemming from the climax. For instance, the denouement in a mystery story usually clarifies all of the evidence and events which have accumulated during the story. Similarly, the last chapter in some novels is used to indicate what happens to all of the characters. In the final chapter of *The Scarlet Letter*, after the climactic scene of Dimmesdale's confession on the scaffold, Hawthorne comments on the fate of each of his characters and at the same time stresses the symbolism of the letter *A.* (See pp. 20-21 for a discussion of a similar use of denouement in "The Ambitious Guest.")

In some stories (especially modern ones), authors deliberately omit denouement to maintain ambiguity—that is, to leave the narrative and its implications incomplete and thus open to various interpretations or speculations. (See pp. 21-23 and *Ambiguity.*)

Dialog is the conversation between people in poetry, plays, and stories. Since dialog is a vital form of action related to plot, it is also a basic source of the study of characters and of an author's style. Although important in all types of literature, dialog is perhaps most crucial for drama, which must rely heavily upon it.

In works which attempt to reconstruct the psychological make-up of man, interior dialog occurs: a character speaks to himself or imagines that he speaks to someone else. In Laura's dream, for example, she visualizes and hears a conversation with Eugenio.

A monolog is one-sided conversation. Two people may be

involved, but one person dominates the conversation, as in "Haircut" and Browning's "My Last Duchess." A soliloquy is a kind of artificial monolog whereby a character in a play expresses to the audience his innermost thoughts and feelings (for example, Hamlet's famous soliloquy "To be or not to be").

In studying dialog in a literary work, the student should bear in mind the following considerations:

1) The relationship of dialog to plot exposition—how well it reveals background information essential to development of action

2) The relationship of dialog to the people uttering it. The dialog may be either close to human speech or highly artificial, but it should be appropriate to the character speaking and to the author's purpose. If handled properly, dialog can establish distinctions among characters and can reveal a great deal about traits, occupations, or social standing.

3) The atmosphere created by the dialog

4) The pace of dialog—the length and complexity of individual speeches or in a play the speed of delivery. The pace can be swift and coherent or extremely slow and involved. Whatever the pace, it should be suitable to the characters and actions at all times.

5) The style of the dialog—prosaic, exalted, emotional, poetic, witty, etc.

Diction signifies the choice and arrangement of words in phrases and images or in larger units such as poetic lines and sentences. Poetic diction has been interpreted as the use of artificial diction to distinguish the language of poetry from that of prose. This distinction, however, is too specialized, for the language of both prose and poetry has an enormous range, from the highly artificial to the representation of real speech patterns. The diction of "To Helen" is, as we have seen, allusive. It also has a grandeur and dignity in such phrases as *barks of yore*. On the other hand, much of the diction of "The Heavy Bear" comes close to contemporary speech. It is important to recognize that the vocabulary current during an author's life will naturally influence his choice of words. Thus it is necessary for a modern student to consult glossaries when reading Shakespeare.

Sometimes an author will deliberately employ archaic words for effect (for example, Spenser in *The Faerie Queene*). In "Ultima Ratio Regum," a modern poem attacking war, Stephen Spender uses the word *silly* to describe his central figure, an anonymous youth destroyed by war and warmongers. The word here does not have the current connotation of *foolish* and *frivolous* but an older meaning of *simple* and *naïve*.

(Since diction is an important part of style, see *Style*.)

Didacticism is the emphasis in a literary work on a thesis, or an overt attempt to instruct or persuade the reader. At its worst, didacticism becomes propaganda: the author pays little attention to technique, and the literary form he uses becomes merely a soapbox for his convictions. An example of direct didacticism is the last paragraph of "The Ambitious Guest"; the whole story, however, is not blatantly didactic, and the moral (the point of instruction) seems to be tacked on.

An example of overt didacticism is Longfellow's "The Village Blacksmith," in which he offers thanks to the blacksmith "for the *lesson* thou hast taught." [Italics mine.] In Longfellow's "Psalm of Life," the reader is addressed directly:

> Let us, then, be up and doing,
> With a heart for any fate;
> Still achieving, still pursuing,
> Learn to labor and to wait.

Many modern writers have swung away from this kind of didacticism. They feel that any moralistic content should be suggested through the technical shaping of the material. "Haircut" (see summary of the story, p. 21) represents this modern approach. Lardner did not choose an omniscient point of view which would allow him to enter the story and make judgments about what occurs, but despite the objectivity of the point of view, the reader reacts to the barber's revelations in the same way that Lardner would. Thus, through a technical achievement and not through direct commentary, Lardner leads his readers to his own evaluation of the barber and Jim.

Frequently students of literature erroneously feel that the meaning of a work can be reduced to a single moral or a point of instruction or advice. This procedure destroys the complexity and vitality of literature by confining it to copybook maxims. If one says that the didactic content of "La Belle Dame" is "Beware of women!" he has completely eliminated the process of interpretation.

Elegy refers to a lyric poem lamenting the death of someone.

A good example is Tennyson's "In Memoriam," a sequence of lyrics on the death of Arthur Hallam. A pastoral elegy has a rural setting with shepherds and nymphs. This kind of elegy has numerous conventions, such as nature joining in the lament or a procession of mourners. Examples are Milton's "Lycidas" and Shelley's "Adonais." In "When Lilacs Last in the Dooryard Bloom'd," Whitman used some of the conventions of the pastoral elegy to lament the death of President Lincoln. Many elegies at their conclusion shift in tone from a sense of despair to a joyous recognition of immortality.

Envelope Pattern (or Enveloping Structure) involves the use of the same or similar words or details at the beginning and end of a literary work. An excellent example is the Knight's repetition in the last stanza of the observer's words in the first stanza of "La Belle Dame sans Merci."

Epic is a long, serious narrative poem written in a grand and elevated style. The narrative concentrates on an heroic and national figure and can encompass vast geographical spaces, national destinies, heaven and hell, and gods and mortals. Although epics tend to be episodic, they maintain some unity through a central hero, conflict, or issue. Epics have numerous conventions, such as beginning *in medias res* (starting a story in the middle), describing in lengthy similes, and offering catalogs of characters. Examples of traditional epics are Homer's *Iliad* and *Odyssey;* examples of literary epics (imitations of the traditional) are Virgil's *Aeneid* and Milton's *Paradise Lost.*

Exposition is that portion of a narrative or drama which provides the necessary background material for a reader or viewer. Exposition establishes setting (time and place); it can create the basic atmosphere; it gives information about the pasts of characters; it provides vital contexts for the events and action which are to unfold. In drama, these must be accomplished by the dialog, particularly in the first or early scenes, or by the stage setting. In other types of literature, especially in the novel, background can be supplied by the author, particularly if he assumes omnisciency. (See pp. 20-21.)

Form and Content The word *form* is sometimes used to designate the organization of a poem. In general it means the shape any literary work assumes as a result of *all* of the technical resources employed by an author. *Content* is the material — ideas, emotions, events, people — which the author is shaping. A fusion of form and content occurs when the author has chosen and successfully worked out the most suitable technical means to develop his subject matter.

Since it is easier to talk about the author's ideas, the emphasis in literary analysis is too often placed upon content; but it is unwise to think of form and content as separate entities. Sonnet 73 and Keats' "On First Looking into Chapman's Homer" are excellent examples of the fusion of form and content, even in terms of the traditions involved. (See *Convention.*) The analysis of the structure of "La Belle Dame" (pp. 16-19) demonstrates the correlation between technique and meaning, and the emphasis on point of view in the essay on "Old Mr. Marblehall" (pp. 72-75) shows how the study of a technique contributes to interpretation or meaning. (See also pp. 23-24 and *Technique.*)

Free Verse designates poetry which breaks from metrical regularity or fixed patterns. Although the verse is free, it generally creates its own internal rhythm. Free verse usually lacks rhyme and frequently unfolds in lengthy lines. For an example of free verse, see the passage from Whitman's "Crossing Brooklyn Ferry," quoted under *Parallelism.*

Genre is the term for a category of literature such as fiction, poetry, and drama. Each type has subdivisions, and in some cases there is an overlapping of the categories to which a particular work may belong. Poetry, for instance, may be used in drama. Some subdivisions for three of the main classifications of literature would be:

Fiction	*Poetry*	*Drama*
Short story	Lyric	Tragedy
Novel	Sonnet	Comedy
	Ode	Melodrama
	Elegy	Farce
	Ballad	
	Epic	

There is sometimes much disagreement about what genre a given work belongs to because some categories are based on form and others on content. For example, a sonnet is classified by form, but an elegy is really distinguished by its content. (See *Convention.*)

Imagery may be considered as either a direct sense appeal and/or a figure of speech which leads a reader to combine at least two elements. A consistent pattern of imagery sometimes constitutes symbolism. (See pp. 7-13.)

Irony is a type of expression which involves opposites or reversals. Since irony most frequently includes relationships of words or actions, it must be analyzed in context. Irony is related to studies of tone, style, point of view, structure, characterization, etc. There are several kinds of irony:

1) Verbal irony — implication of a meaning opposite to a direct statement; or the juxtaposition of words, one set of which cancels out the other. Such a mode of expression might be loosely termed sarcasm. The following sentence from "Flowering Judas" demonstrates the use of words with opposite meanings as well as the canceling out of one set of words by another:

> Braggioni loves himself with such tenderness and amplitude and eternal charity that his followers — for he is a leader of men, a skilled revolutionist, and his skin has been punctured in honorable warfare — warm themselves in the reflected glow, and say to each other: "He has a real nobility, a love of humanity raised above mere personal affections."

The word *skilled* is not to be taken literally; in the context it implies that if Braggioni has skill, it is in his own behalf. The phrase "his skin has been punctured in honorable warfare" suggests sarcastically that Braggioni's concern for himself has never permitted him to engage in serious combat. The concluding statement attributed to the followers is completely canceled out by the opening clause which indicates Braggioni's monstrous egotism.

2) Irony of situation — the reversal of events, the backfiring of events, or the canceling of one action or detail by another. These reversals may be due to forces beyond the control of characters, to the actions and mistakes of people, to coincidence, or to the manipulations of an omniscient author. The reversal is frequently not expected by those involved; for example, Oedipus seeks a murderer who turns out to be himself. In "The Ambitious Guest," a quirk of fate, of natural forces beyond the control of the family, denies their expectation of safety in the shelter which they have prepared. In "Haircut," Paul, who had been the butt of Jim's jokes, reverses the situation by killing Jim. An example of an omniscient author's manipulation of

events and details occurs in "Old Mr. Marblehall." While the old man excitedly awaits the day of the revelation of his second life to the community, Miss Welty pointedly depicts the utter indifference of the town.

3) Irony of character — reversals of expected patterns of behavior in characters; related, of course, to irony of situation. If Laura were to shoot Braggioni, or if Braggioni were to magnanimously renounce his pursuit of Laura, the anticipated behavior of the characters would have been turned around. If such a reversal of character occurs, the author must make the change credible. In "Haircut," the reader has been prepared for Paul's shift to aggressive action because he has been told of the half-wit's devotion to Julie and Doc. In "The Short Happy Life of Francis Macomber" by Hemingway, Macomber's sudden reversion from cowardice to courage is made plausible by his anger over his wife's adultery.

4) Dramatic irony — a character operates without the awareness which a reader or observer has of his plight or of his limited knowledge. One of the most famous examples in literature is Oedipus. Although usually found in drama, dramatic irony can appear in other narratives.

(See also *Paradox* and *Understatement.*)

Literal Meaning and Figurative Meaning *Literal meaning* appears only on the surface of a literary work and is represented by an emphasis on denotation, summary, and paraphrase. *Figurative meaning* is suggested by the connotations of words and by the images employed by an author. When these meanings are put together and analyzed, one goes beneath the surface of a story or poem and in effect interprets it.

An example of literal meaning is the following paraphrase of "On First Looking into Chapman's Homer":

I have traveled much in golden kingdoms. I have been to western islands with which poets loyal to Apollo are associated. One of those about whom I have heard much is Homer. I did not enjoy his work until I read Chapman's translation. During that experience I felt like an astronomer seeing a new planet or like Cortez and his men when they discovered the Pacific.

For an analysis of the figurative implications of the poem, see the essay on pages 56-58. Figurative meaning is also an important part of the emphasis on analytical reading in Chapter 1.

Lyric is a poem, generally short, presented by a single speaker, either the poet or some voice imaginatively adopted by the poet, and expressing some basic emotion such as sorrow or love. The tone can vary from a light frivolous compliment to a beloved one to a deeply felt yearning or sorrow. Lyrics are generally tightly constructed with a unity of a single mood, emotion, and/or thought. Poe's "To Helen" is an excellent example of a lyric. Sonnets are a kind of lyric; elegies and odes are longer and more complex lyrics.

Melodrama denotes a form of drama or narrative in which superficial characters are depicted engaging in sensational events. Hence melodrama is an extreme distortion of reality. As such, it is frequently sentimental and didactic in that it draws sharp distinctions between heroes and villains (as in Westerns on television). Its purpose is to affect the emotions rather than to stimulate thought.

Sometimes in the midst of a serious literary work, especially plays, an author will intrude melodramatic events for effect. One then has to decide whether the intrusion fits the rest of the work or violates its spirit. Actually the rapid multiple slaughters at the end of *Hamlet* are melodramatic; however, in the context of the whole play and the development of Hamlet's character, the melodrama does not destroy the tragic effect.

Metaphor is a figure of speech in which one element substitutes for another. The substitution may be implied or direct. (See pp. 9-11.)

Meter denotes the measured pattern of stressed and unstressed syllables in a line of poetry. A stressed syllable can be marked ´, and an unstressed syllable can be designated ˘. The combinations of these syllables are generally measured in feet. Among the most important metrical feet are the following:

    Iamb ˘ ´
    When I consider how my light is spent
                    John Milton

    Trochee ´ ˘
    Maid of Athens, ere we part,

    Give, oh give me back my heart!
                    Byron

(Note the extra stressed monosyllabic word at the end of each line.)
Anapest ˘ ˘ /

And the widows of Ashur are loud in their wail,

And the idols are broke in the temple of Baal

Byron

Dactyl / ˘ ˘

This is the forest primeval. The murmuring pines and

the hemlocks

Longfellow

(Note the incomplete dactyl, or trochee, at the end of the line.)

A line of one foot is called monometer; two, dimeter; three, trimeter; four, tetrameter; five, pentameter; six, hexameter. For example, Milton's line would be iambic pentameter, and Longfellow's dactylic hexameter. Iambic pentameter is perhaps the most commonly used metrical line in English.

Regularity of metrical patterns is not necessarily a sign of good poetry; in fact, too much regularity can create monotony. Hence a poet can vary metrical patterns in several ways:

1) By adding a syllable at the end of a line (an unstressed syllable being considered a feminine ending; a stressed syllable, a masculine ending)

2) By stressing two syllables consecutively and creating a spondee (//)

3) By mixing in other patterns and yet maintaining a dominant one; for example, an occasional trochee in an iambic pattern

In addition, pauses and the dramatic stresses involved in rhetorical and meaningful oral reading of poetry can alter the emphasis in the pattern of scanned (marked by symbols) metrics. In fact, many students of literature feel that the metrical feet referred to above are artificially imposed on English poetry by practices in classical Latin verse, for which they are far more suitable. Many also feel that scanning poetry can become a pedantic exercise if one does not pay attention to the infinite musical and rhetorical possibilities of poetry. For example, one would not expect every actor to recite "To be or not to be" in exactly the same way despite the seeming regularity of the iambic meter. Instead of being concerned solely with the scansion of "To-morrow, and to-morrow and to-morrow," one would perhaps be wiser to recognize the long and slow unfolding of the music of the line to designate the tortuous progress of human experience toward a meaningless future extinction.

Motif is a repeated word, phrase, or action or variations of these. Motifs can be related to characterization, emphasizing a person's mannerisms, appearance, or traits. Motifs contribute to both content and structure because they are meaningful threads which run through a literary work and thus help unify it. In "The Ambitious Guest," the wind, the falling rocks, and the persistent references to death are motifs foreshadowing the climax of the story. In "Flowering Judas," the references to Braggioni's playing a guitar may be said to constitute a motif. The way he plays and sings and the way he holds the guitar (at one point practically strangling it) contribute to the unflattering characterization of the revolutionist. The repetition of indefinite pronouns like *nobody* and *everybody* in "Old Mr. Marblehall" is a motif reflecting the town's indifference. If dominant enough, a motif, like a pattern of imagery, can be considered symbolical. Thus it is possible to see the numerous references to Braggioni's bulk as a symbol of his piggish exploitation of the revolution.

Myth may be defined as a motif or narrative recurring through human experience and religious history and dealing with gods or heroes, with natural phenomena, or with basic hopes and fears of people derived from universal experience and transformed into psychological or imaginative expression. A myth thus is a part of the cultural and religious heritage of mankind.

There are many sources of myth which literary artists have used:

1) Anthropology—primitive rites of initiation and trial (the experience of Francis Macomber in Hemingway's story and of Ike McCaslin in Faulkner's "The Bear")

2) Natural phenomena—water as purification, spring as rebirth

3) A given culture—cultural mythology and works like the *Iliad* and *Oedipus the King*. Poe uses classical myth in "To Helen." An example of a modern adaptation of classical mythology is Eugene O'Neill's *Mourning Becomes Electra*.

4) A given religion—for example, the Judas tree, the fall of Adam and Eve

5) Psychology—the Oedipus complex as representative of man's incestuous desire (Freud), or archetypes, which are ele-

ments of human experience residing permanently in the collective unconscious of man, such as death and rebirth or the struggle between generations.

Instead of adapting the ancient myths, some authors have created their legendary world with its own system of symbols and values. Blake and Yeats are examples of such myth-making authors, and it has been argued that Faulkner's Yoknapatawpha County represents such a mythical domain in American literature.

If an author does not create his own mythological apparatus, he will frequently draw upon the human storehouse of attitudes, beliefs, and stories and adapt them to his own intentions. Then the student of literature must study the mythological implications in the context of the literary work. Myth in a literary work becomes an allusion. If the mythical material is extensively employed, then it can become highly symbolical.

Although one has to guard against finding a myth lurking in every line of a literary work, his awareness of this vast reservoir of cultural heritage can help him interpret many stories, poems, and plays.

Ode is a long lyric poem, generally free in structure but usually serious in subject matter, which can be quite varied. The style of an ode is dignified and rhetorical. Some famous examples are Wordsworth's "Ode on Intimations of Immortality" and Keats' "Ode on a Grecian Urn."

Onomatopoeia is the use of a word or words which imitate the sound they stand for. Some examples are *hiss, hum, buzz, murmur.*

Paradox is the linking of ideas or feelings which are seemingly contradictory but which actually express a basic truth when they are put together and the implications are formulated. Paradox is related to irony. Shakespeare's Sonnet 73 is a good example of paradox. (See pp. 99-101.) Another example of paradox is found in the actions of Ahab in *Moby Dick:* in his zeal to destroy evil as represented in the whale, Ahab commits evil.

Parallelism denotes the balancing of equal parts of a sentence, the repetition of a sentence pattern, or the repetition of words at the beginning of lines of poetry. When an author frequently stresses the equal parts of sentences, the word *balance* is used to describe his style. This is characteristic of some of the prose of the King James version of the Bible. Such use of parallelism contributes to the musical quality of prose or poetry. An example of considerable use of parallelism in poetry is the following passage from Whitman's "Crossing Brooklyn Ferry":

> Others will enter the gates of the ferry and cross from shore to shore,
> Others will watch the run of the flood-tide,
> Others will see the shipping of Manhattan north and west, and the heights of Brooklyn to the south and east,
> Others will see the islands large and small;
> Fifty years hence, others will see them as they cross, the sun half an hour high,
> A hundred years hence, or ever so many hundred years hence, others will see them,
> Will enjoy the sunset, the pouring-in of the flood-tide, the falling back to the sea of the ebb-tide.

Personification may be defined as the giving of human characteristics or shape to an inanimate object, to an emotion or instinct, to a moral quality, to an event like death, or to an invisible essence like the soul. (See p. 9.)

Plot consists of the story or narrative which depicts a unified or purposeful sequence of events or which meaningfully relates events and details disconnected in time. The events in a plot can be told about, or they can be portrayed dramatically, as through the dialog of characters. The angle from which they are told is the point of view. The organization of the events and everything connected with them is plot structure (see pp. 20-23). Plot is always related to characterization, for the thoughts, words, and actions of people contribute to the nature of, and the relationships between, events. A plot may be highly complex, as in a mystery story or in some novels, or a narrative may be relatively plotless because little action seems to occur. As a general rule, plot in a short story tends to be far less complex than that in a novel because the short story writer is restricted, of course, by limitations of space.

Point of View may be defined as the angle or perspective from which a story is told or from which a poet speaks. Behind every point of view stands the author; and the differences among the kinds of point of view come from the degree of intrusion by the author in telling his story. There are basically two general types of point of view—that in which the author is in some way directly present, telling and even commenting on the narrative, and that in which the author turns over the story to a narrator, whom he, of course, creates.

Among the author points of view (generally told in the third person) three are important:

1) Omniscient author—the author is definitely telling the story, manipulating events, shifting his perspective from one character to another, making comments about what is going on, and/or creating a definite tone which reveals his attitude toward the events, people, and concepts which he has created. In short, the author chooses whatever perspective he wants at any time in the narrative. In "The Ambitious Guest," Hawthorne is obviously present, even to the extent of directly moralizing about the guest at the end. In "Flowering Judas," Miss Porter tells a great deal about the backgrounds of Laura and Braggioni and reveals her attitudes toward them. In addition to telling about Laura, Miss Porter takes the reader into Laura's consciousness—her inner life—by means of the dream. (For a discussion of the omniscient perspective, one should refer to the analysis of "Old Mr. Marblehall" on pp. 72-75.)

2) Limited omniscience—the author tells the story by focusing on a central character and filtering most or all of the story through the chosen consciousness. The character's responses to what is going on make him a reflector. His reflections may be based on varying degrees of awareness, ranging from the naïve to the most acute. Within this kind of point of view the author can still analyze and comment, but he confines himself to the impact of events on the character he has chosen as the central consciousness. Thus the presentation seems more objective than that of full omnisciency. The best examples of this use of point of view can be found in stories and novels by Henry James such as "The Liar" and *The Ambassadors*.

3) Dramatic point of view—like a dramatist, the author tells the story by putting his characters into action and building his story around their dialog. He has to designate their physical action or movements and establish setting and description, but for the most part the characters perform as if they were on the stage. Of the three author points of view, this is the most objective in that the author is most removed from the story. A famous example of this kind of storytelling is Hemingway's "The Killers," which consists largely of dialog.

When the author allows a narrator to tell the story, he steps aside so that the created character may perform. In dealing with a narrator, the author usually has to maintain stricter control of his material than he would if he were fully omniscient. He cannot comment directly. Logic demands that the narrator should be naturally aware of what happens. If the narrator is told about events and does not directly observe or participate in them, the circumstances of his receiving information cannot be strained or illogical. Essentially there are three ways in which an author can employ a narrator, who generally tells the story in the first person:

1) The narrator who participates only as an observer. He may or may not react to the people and events he observes. In "Birthday Party," the narrator does react to the events. The whole meaning of the story has to come from the narrator, who does not know the husband and wife whose actions are under observation.

2) The narrator who observes and participates in the action. He becomes an important character in his own right, but is not necessarily the chief character. In effect, he tells somebody else's story which has had a profound impact upon his life or concepts. As opposed to the narrator of "Birthday Party," this kind of narrator becomes a personality which the reader can analyze. The barber in "Haircut" participates to some extent in the activities which he is recounting. Although he is telling Jim Kendall's story, he reveals a great deal about himself and about his own inability to perceive what has happened. Fitzgerald's *The Great Gatsby* and Warren's *All the King's Men* are excellent examples of narrated stories wherein the narrators are significant observers and participators.

3) The narrator who tells his own story. In doing so, he reveals his basic character. In a sense the barber in "Haircut" belongs in this category too, for he unconsciously reveals his own character and at the same time damns Jim, whose malicious actions he is trying to condone. In this example, the point of view provides a great deal of irony. In contrast to the barber is Huck Finn, who tells his story so innocently and candidly that the reader is impelled to see and judge events by his standards.

In analyzing narrative, one must determine the point of view because it can lead him to consider numerous aspects of an author's technique: tone, style, characterization, and plot structure.

In a narrative poem the poet can assume omnisciency; in a dramatic monolog the speaker is like a narrator in a story. However, since lyric poetry speaks directly to a reader and frequently employs the pronoun *I,* one has to decide whether the speaker is the poet himself or whether he is exercising his freedom to speak in any voice he chooses. In regard to Poe's "To Helen" and Keats' "On First Looking into Chapman's Homer," research would indicate that the poets are speaking as individuals but at the same time offering a description of experiences which others may have had. In "The Heavy Bear," one cannot assume that the *I* is Delmore Schwartz. In fact, the last two lines would indicate that the poet has adopted the voice of man and is describing a conflict common to all.

In drama, point of view is not vital, unless there is a narrator in a play (for example, Wilder's *Our Town* and Williams' *The Glass Menagerie*). A dramatist has to bring characters alive through dialog and actions and cannot intrude his own commentary or omnisciency except in stage directions. He will clearly focus on his chief characters, but they have to convey the situations and meanings. See dramatic point of view above.

Rhyme is the use of matching sounds, generally accented vowels, at the end of two lines or more of poetry. For example, in the first stanza of "To Helen," *me* rhymes with *sea,* and *yore* with *bore* and *shore.* In some lines of poetry, a syllable or more after the accented vowel will also correspond — for example, such terminal words as *tarry* and *carry, growing* and *sowing.*

Sight (or eye) rhyme occurs when two words look alike but do not sound alike — for instance, *love-prove.* Sometimes such rhyming words may have been pronounced the same way at the time the poet used them (*wind-kind*).

Slant rhyme occurs when an author avoids perfect rhyme and creates only a partial correspondence between words. In the second stanza of "To Helen," *face* and *Greece* should perhaps be considered a slant rhyme.

A rhyme scheme is the pattern of rhyme in a stanza or in an entire poem. To designate the pattern of rhyme in a poem, one usually uses lower case letters of the alphabet starting with *a* and changing the letter for each new rhyme. Thus the rhyme scheme of the first stanza of Poe's "To Helen" would be *ababb.* One should realize that in English poetry there are numerous stanza forms with established rhyme schemes — for example, the ballad stanza, which rhymes *abcb.* See also *Sonnet.*

An internal rhyme occurs when words within one line of poetry rhyme or when nonterminal words within two lines rhyme. In the following stanza from "The Rime of the Ancient

Mariner," one can note two examples of internal rhyme:

> The fair breeze *blew,* the white foam *flew,*
> The furrow followed free;
> We were the *first* that ever *burst*
> Into that silent sea.

The passage above also contains alliteration, assonance, and consonance (see separate entries), which some students of literature consider rhyme.

Rhyme of any kind obviously contributes to the musical quality of poetry. Although it can impose on a poet limited choices of words and although it can sometimes create a monotonous pattern of sound, rhyme has been effectively used in many poems. It is perhaps most effective when it contributes not only to sound but also to the development of meaning and mood. It is perhaps least effective when words are arbitrarily or artificially chosen to match sounds or when the placement of the rhyming words distorts the natural word order or syntax of a poetic sentence.

Rhythm is the measured movement or beat in the musical flow of poetry established by the technical resources of both the poet and the oral interpreter of his work. Although sometimes associated solely with the alternating stresses or beats of meter, rhythm is really created by many factors involved in the reading of poetry. In addition to meter, such elements as pauses, speed of delivery, intonation of voice, and volume of sound can contribute to the rhythmical pulsations of poetry.

Since rhythm is really larger than meter, the measured foot of meter is not the sole criterion of establishing rhythm. For example, the phrasing or the grammatical groupings of words, which could possibly contain numerous measured feet, condition rhythm considerably.

Although generally related to poetry, rhythm is also applicable to prose, as the King James version of the Bible amply illustrates. In some prose the rhythm is so pronounced that it is impossible to draw a dividing line between poetry and prose.

Run-on Line (Enjambement) is the continuation of the thought and structure of a poetic sentence from one line to the next without pause. A line in which thought and structure conclude simultaneously is referred to as end-stopped, as in the second line of the closed couplet. The run-on line provides flexibility and parallels human discourse more truly than the end-stopped couplet does.

Within the limitations of the closed couplet, the first line can progress structurally to the second as in the following from Pope's "Moral Essay Four":

> 'Tis strange, the miser should his cares employ
> To gain those riches he can ne'er enjoy:
> Is it less strange, the prodigal should waste
> His wealth, to purchase what he ne'er can taste?

In the following passage from Arnold's "Dover Beach," the flexibility of run-on lines is apparent:

> Sophocles long ago
> Heard it on the Aegean, and it brought
> Into his mind the turbid ebb and flow
> Of human misery; we
> Find also in the sound a thought,
> Hearing it by this distant northern sea.

Satire designates criticism of a person, human nature, events, movements, or institutions. It uses techniques of exaggeration, ridicule, sarcasm, irony, humor, and of reducing some person or situation to absurdity. It can range in degree from gentle needling to fierce swinging of baseball bats. In the first book of *Gulliver's Travels,* Swift employs the Lilliputians to satirize the pettiness of human nature and the political disputes of his own day. In "A Modest Proposal," he uses irony to condemn those who keep the Irish in poverty. When he suggests that the bodies of babies can be used as a table delicacy and hence as a source of income for their parents, he is not to be taken literally. The exaggerated irony is devastating. In *Huckleberry Finn,* there is a great deal of satire — for example, the conversation between Huck and Jim about kings and the portrayal of the confidence man in the Duke and the Dauphin.

Setting designates the place and time of the events of a plot, either in prose or poetry. Setting helps create atmosphere, the mood radiating from a given environment. In some works one will find an immediate setting placed in a larger context. In "Flowering Judas," the immediate settings are Laura's dwelling and Braggioni's home, but these are always placed in the larger setting of the revolution. In "Haircut," the barber shop (the immediate setting) in a small-town environment (the larger context) is a suitable place for the garrulous, gossipy barber and for the audience which seems to relish the malicious activities of Jim. Mr. Marblehall's two existences, one real and the other imagined, are a basic part of the town, not only in terms of geographical location but also in terms of conflict.

Setting can enter into other aspects of analysis. For instance, it can be important in a study of plot structure, especially if the scene shifts a great deal, as it does in *Huckleberry Finn*. It can also be significant if one is analyzing a character as affected by or in conflict with his environment (Laura in the midst of the Mexican revolution). Since settings usually have to be described by an author, his power of description is relevant to a study of style. Frequently setting can also serve a symbolical purpose, as, for example, the grot and the cold hill's side in "La Belle Dame" or the fissure (crack) in the house of Usher, which symbolically foreshadows the physical destruction of the house and the disintegration of the Usher line.

Although in some poems setting is not too important, one cannot neglect it in studying poetry. In a narrative poem like "The Ancient Mariner," the descriptions of settings are essential in making a supernatural sequence of events seem real. In a lyric poem like Wordsworth's sonnet "Composed on Westminster Bridge," the setting is the basis of the poet's recorded response. Wordsworth describes his reactions to his view of London from the bridge early in the morning.

In drama the playwright usually records his concept of settings in stage directions or in dialog, and the designer translates these into his own artistic version.

(See p. 20 for further discussion of setting. See also *Exposition.*)

Simile is a figure of speech which makes a direct comparison between two elements and which is usually introduced by *like* or *as*. (See pp. 8-9.)

Sonnet is generally a fourteen-line lyric which uses any one of several different rhyme schemes. The Italian or Petrarchan sonnet is divided into an eight-line unit (octave) and a concluding six-line part (sestet). The octave rhymes *abba abba,* and the sestet is sometimes *cde cde* or some variation. The English or

Shakespearean sonnet consists of three four-line sections (quatrains) and one couplet, rhyming *abab cdcd efef gg*. Although there are other variations, the sonnet is generally a tightly concentrated form of poetry. (See *Convention*.)

Stanza refers to the arrangement of a group of poetic lines into a pattern generally suggested by a rhyme scheme. The pattern is often repeated. "To Helen" is divided into three stanzas with a subtly varied rhyme scheme of *ababb; cdcdc; effef*. See also *Sonnet*.

Stanzas are roughly the equivalent of paragraphs in prose. In fact, when a unit within a poem does not have a formal stanzaic pattern, it can be called a verse paragraph. One may say that "The Heavy Bear" is divided into three verse paragraphs.

Stream of Consciousness is the term used to describe an author's representation of the flow of inner thoughts, feelings, and memories of a character, regardless of logical order and transitions. This approach is based on the assumption that our half-conscious and even conscious thoughts and feelings do not come to us in neat patterns or in carefully constructed plots. Free association, which is used in a simple way in "Haircut," is a basis of stream of consciousness; that is, one thought or feeling is almost automatically associated with the next one. Despite the seeming chaos of stream of consciousness, there can be a sense of unity through the depiction of dominant emotions or fears or through the establishment of an environment or context (the structure of myth in Joyce's *Ulysses*) which controls inner turbulence.

As a technique, stream of consciousness derives from the transference of psychological knowledge to the artistic creation of the inner man. For this reason it provides the author and the reader with the most complex and penetrating means of characterization. Some critics consider stream of consciousness a point of view — a perspective whereby an author allows us to look *inside* a character. Stream of consciousness is also relevant to a study of style, especially since it is not likely to provide orderly sentence patterns or easily decipherable diction. Finally, as implied, stream of consciousness is also related to structure. In analysis of this kind of structure, we must apply psychological knowledge as well as some of the literary approaches to structure (motifs or symbols, for example).

Occasionally an author will use limited stream of consciousness in the midst of an orderly narrative. An example of this technique is Laura's dream.

Stress is the emphasis placed upon syllables which are more dominant than others. The emphasis is generally based on a common or accepted pronunciation of a word; however, the sense of a word, its position in a line, or the rhetorical necessities involved in reading poetry aloud may alter the accepted (or dictionary) stress patterns among the syllables. Stressing syllables to accommodate the meaning or emotional content of a poem is probably more important than forcing stresses to fit metrical patterns prevailing in a poem. See *Meter.*

Structure signifies the basic organization or arrangement of events, details, words, or parts (chapter, stanza, scene, for example) in a literary work. For a discussion of the structure of poetry and fiction, see pages 13-23.

Analysis of the unity of drama will involve some of the approaches to stories, since it is essentially narrative. However, there is one special aspect of the structure of drama that needs to be pointed out—the emphasis on scenes and the relationship among them (scenic construction). Because the dramatist must limit and select carefully the actions which will be portrayed, he emphasizes the scene or the act as his unit of structure. The fact that the curtain will fall between scenes and acts will frequently cause a playwright to seek climactic or high moments for the end of each unit. Sometimes within a scene or act, the entrances and exits of characters create smaller divisions of action (as in the first act of Ibsen's *Hedda Gabler*). Despite these special aspects of dramatic structure, all of the parts of a play should build to a coherent unit which indicates the author's purpose. An excellent example of dramatic structure is *Oedipus the King*. In comedy, of course, the structural unity of plot is sometimes sacrificed so that the individual parts can evoke laughter.

Style can be defined as the author's selection and arrangement of words used in presenting his imaginative creation. Although every author has *a* style, the reader would be wise to analyze the style of each work that he reads, especially if the author is known for his experimentation in style (Faulkner, for instance). He should determine whether the author is allowing a dazzling style to substitute for meaningful content. In addition, a reader must recognize that an author's style can be influenced by the vocabulary and stylistic modes of his times.

A close study of style in both prose and poetry involves numerous factors:

1) Diction — the author's vocabulary or choice of words. The reader can determine whether the author's usage is vague or concrete, vivid and vigorous or turgid and dull, denotative or connotative, conversational or unusual, archaic, artificial and/or ornate.

2) Sentence patterns — the arrangement of words into sentences. Relevant to this problem are such things as the simplicity or complexity of the sentences, the balance of the parts, parallelism, syntax, periodic and loose sentences.

3) Use of sense impressions, description, and figures of speech.

4) Fluency — the smooth movement from one sentence and one paragraph to another, or from line to line in poetry, guiding the reader gently by means of transitions. Sometimes, of course, an author will be deliberately incoherent, especially if he is depicting the inner confusions of a character.

5) Economy or expansiveness in use of words and details. One should remember that compression is generally characteristic of poetry.

6) Tone — the author's attitude which is apparent because of his choice of words or his arrangement of details. Involved are such attitudes as the ironic, satiric, objective, pessimistic, cynical, optimistic, comic, or tragic.

7) Use of dialog — one can determine whether the dialog is stilted or artificial, natural, or witty, and whether it is appropriate to the characters who speak.

8) Sound or musical quality — although sound is an important part of poetry, style in prose fiction can also involve a study of sounds.

9) Miscellaneous — use of puns (play on words) or allusions.

One should evaluate the appropriateness of the style in relation to the content of a given work. As an example of the study of style, let us examine "Old Mr. Marblehall" and "The Heavy Bear."

In "Old Mr. Marblehall," Miss Welty's tone is frequently revealed by stylistic devices. She uses very concrete details and images which emphasize the bizarre and the blurred. In addition, the details establish contrasts which heighten the effects the author wishes to achieve. For example, Marblehall's son is at first compared to a staring kitten; later his penetrating look is described as monkeylike. The shift in the imagery stresses his bizarre nature. These images are surrounded by some extremely concrete descriptive details. The reader is not too concerned about the boy's "button nose" or his "tiny little pearl teeth." On the other hand, details that fix upon his "pointed ears," "his very sparse Japanese hair," and especially his "long wilted fingers" stress the abnormality of the child and underscore Miss Welty's somewhat amused attitude toward the unnatural fruit of the Marblehalls' late union.

The description of Marblehall's second environment also plays up opposites which make it seem weird. The mazelike streets of the neighborhood and the "little galleried houses nearly alike" establish the environment as a kind of blur to which nobody pays any attention because nothing has individual identity. Yet in the midst of this blur, there is an emphasis on vivid noises: the whirring screen doors, "the ice wagons dragging by," and "the twittering" of the children. The most outstanding noise stresses the painful anonymity of the residents' existence: the radio which "seems to mourn and cry for them." In the midst of these vividly portrayed noises lies a dead existence. Even when Marblehall and his zinnias emerge from the anonymity, the ever-present dust blurs the picture. Since this environment is part of Marblehall's fantasy, the stressing of death and dust reflect Miss Welty's unsympathetic depiction of the failure of Marblehall's fantasy.

By analyzing the individual descriptive details and their relationships to one another, one can determine that the author's style clearly contributes to her tone and hence to the basic meaning of the story.

"The Heavy Bear" represents an adaptation of style to a different purpose and a different genre (poetry). One notices first that the style of the poem is characterized by long and involved sentences. Stanzas one and three consist of one sentence each, and in both the syntax is extremely complicated. For instance, in stanza one the subject of the sentence appears in line one and the verbs in lines 8 and 9. Between subject and predicate in this rather lengthy stanza are a series of modifiers and several appositives of the subject. The syntax of stanza three is even more complicated, with appositives still predominant. Here the subject is complemented by a series of nine verbs, most of which begin lines (*Has followed, Moves, Perplexes, Stretches, Touches,* and *Stumbles*). In view of such involved syntax, it seems highly likely that the author created his poetic sentences so that their complexity would reflect the clumsy movement of the bear.

Suspense is the means used by an author to keep the interest of his readers or audience in what is happening or in the results of what has happened to the people in his narrative. An author can employ the following means to maintain suspense: he can make his characters so compelling that one becomes anxious about the outcome of their experiences; he can construct his plot so that the final resolution or climax is withheld until the end of the story; he can foreshadow or suggest an outcome subtly and at the same time keep his readers curious and anxious; he can provide a surprise ending contrary to the expectations of a reader, who nevertheless recognizes it as a logical outcome of preceding events. In "The Ambitious Guest," for example, Hawthorne foreshadows the climax and yet does not completely reveal the freak nature of the slide until it happens. The foreshadowing occurs in the numerous references to winds, falling stones, and death.

Sometimes an outcome is clear to a reader and yet he is completely enthralled by the unfolding of events. This element of suspense can be based on natural curiosity; in "Haircut," we learn early in the story that Jim Kendall is dead, but we do not discover why and how he died until the events emerge from the barber's rambling account. Our desire to know helps Lardner establish a suspense which becomes even keener because of the piecemeal revelation. In *Oedipus the King*, we can sense the outcome of Oedipus' plight, yet the suspenseful fascination comes from observing his own actions push him unknowingly to his downfall.

Symbol is a fusion of two entities: one (the symbol itself) usually has some concrete form, and the other is essentially the abstract concept or meaning which the symbol represents in the context of a literary work. (See pp. 11-13.)

The following diagram with its emphasis on the means one uses to explain a symbol may be of help to a student:

| *Symbol* | The naked bulb in "Old Mr. Marble-hall" |

Means by Which One Analyzes the Symbol	Close analysis of context; out of context the bulb is not a symbol. Analysis includes the relationship between the two appearances of the bulb (structure); the relevance of the bulb to Marblehall's reading and his psychological make-up (characterization); linking the bulb to the author's attitude toward Marblehall (tone and point of view)
Suggested Meaning of the Symbol	The ironic light of reality which reveals that Marblehall's reading has stimulated a vivid but futile fantasy

Technique signifies any resources or any combination of means used by an author to shape his material, such as his choice and arrangement of words (style), his organization of his material (structure), or his handling of characters (characterization).

Theme is the essential meaning or main concepts of a literary work. (In this text the word is also used to designate an essay written by a student.) In literary analysis, too much attention to capturing the theme of a work can reduce it to utter simplicity. For example, if one says that the theme of "The Ambitious Guest" is the futility of excessive pride, he will not get much from the story. He would be wiser to examine the many implications of the meaning of the story and the means employed by Hawthorne to develop his ideas. (See the analysis of the story on pp. 104-109.)

Tone consists of the author's basic attitude toward the people, situations, emotions, and/or ideas with which he has constructed his literary work. In addition, the author's attitude toward his audience can be considered tone.

Authors can employ numerous general and specific tones. Some general adjectives which can be used to describe tone are pessimistic, cynical, ironic, optimistic, objective, satiric, comic, and tragic. Sometimes the author will mix tones in one work. When a mixture occurs, one should try to determine whether the change is logical or purposeful.

Analysis of tone requires a careful study of technique. Tone is related to point of view, especially the omniscient perspective. However, if an objective point of view or a narrator is employed, one cannot easily relate the author's attitude to his subject matter. An author's manipulation of events in a plot can possibly reveal his tone. In a study of character, one should attempt to determine whether the author reveals his own attitude toward the fictional person as Miss Porter does toward Braggioni in "Flowering Judas." Tone is also related to style; for example, irony and sarcasm definitely influence an author's choice of words. Sometimes, especially for lyric poetry, research will help one establish whether the author speaks for himself or whether he has projected an imagined voice.

Several works reprinted in this volume will illustrate tone. As we have seen, the tone of "Flowering Judas" is frequently ironic. In "The Heavy Bear," one detects a tone of pessimism or frustration produced by a feeling of powerlessness against the animal urges of man. In the sonnet "On First Looking into Chapman's Homer" the tone of awe and wonder is effectively communicated to a reader. See also *Style.*

Tragedy Ever since Aristotle attempted to describe and define Greek tragedy in his incomplete *Poetics*, there have been numerous attempts to pin down what the word means. Needless to say, much dispute has occurred. Since tragedy is an important kind of drama and since characters in stories and novels can be discussed as tragic figures, we need to understand some of the possible characteristics of tragedy.

The tone of the tragedian must be serious. Although he may introduce comic relief to lessen the tension of tragic circumstances (as in the grave-diggers scene in *Hamlet*), he cannot be frivolous, sarcastic, or satirical. The people and events of tragedy should relate to important human problems—a man's relationship to his fellow man, to the social order, to fate, or to his God. In this connection one should note that the seriousness of much tragedy stems from the family unit, the most vital context for man—for example, Oedipus' unintentional acts of murdering his father and marrying his mother; Hamlet's struggles with his uncle and stepfather, Claudius; and Willy Loman's influence on his sons in *Death of a Salesman.*

The nature of the protagonist or hero in tragedy is most important. Generally tragedy focuses on a central figure whose plight is significant enough to engage the attention of his audience. In Greek tragedy the hero is a legendary figure or a ruler, a person of high socio-political status; in Shakespearean tragedy he is invariably a king, a prince, or a warrior. However, with the advent of democratic societies, the protagonist cannot belong to royalty.

Usually the tragic hero is not perfect; in fact, his downfall stems from some flaw or error of judgment. However, he usually is a good enough human being to warrant the sympathy of an audience. Influenced by the advance in psychology, some modern playwrights create complex characters whose flaws and errors cannot be easily isolated.

The circumstances which constitute the plot of a tragedy are centered on the tragic figure, the people he influences, and/or his adversaries. Aristotle insisted upon a unified plot with a beginning, middle, and ending. Although Shakespeare was more interested in characterization than in plot structure, he invariably focuses on his central figure or figures, and when he introduces a subplot as in *King Lear*, he has both dramatic and thematic justification. Even the psychological plot structure of *Death of a Salesman* has considerable unity.

The circumstances of a tragedy must contain conflict, both internal and external. The conflict means struggle. Most students of tragedy feel that its spirit is basically represented when man demonstrates his dignity and higher potentialities in the midst of his struggles, even those that destroy him. Because classical tragedy emphasizes this dignity of man, many contemporary plays are not considered tragedies. However, some modern critics feel that it is no longer possible to portray man as dignified in his struggles, and they argue that man's capacity to cling to his beliefs, no matter how wrong, or to endure, no matter how undignified the hero may be, constitutes tragedy.

The outcome of the struggle is usually catastrophic, though it is wrong to say that tragedy must end with the death of the central figure. Oedipus' act of piercing his eyes may be a worse fate than death. According to Aristotle, reversal of fortune and recognition of one's plight or mistakes is essential to the outcome and to the structure of the plot. He cited *Oedipus the King* as an excellent example of such a plot.

Although one may feel a sense of waste in the results of a tragedy, a sense of order — cosmic, moral, or social — is frequently maintained. Oedipus seems to be a victim of a cosmic order — fate and the gods — which encompasses him and to which he submits. In *Hamlet* political order is re-established by Fortinbras after the destruction of the hero and Claudius. Some modern tragedians feel that the sense of order is not part of contemporary life; hence the outcome of tragedy to them involves chaos, not order. In addition, they feel that amidst the chaos the tragic figure should not be expected to recognize either himself or his surroundings. In fact, the proponents of modern tragedy might argue that the real tragedy of present-day life is the inability of man to perceive or to penetrate the chaos around him. For this reason, characters whom Eugene O'Neill would consider tragic pursue perpetual pipe dreams and hence never understand themselves.

Aristotle used the word *catharsis* to describe the effect of tragedy on an audience. Although there is little agreement about what Aristotle really meant, he apparently felt that tragedy purges its viewers of pity and fear and lifts them to an elevated state—a sense of harmony with the tragic experience, or an awareness of the great capacity and potentialities of man. Since some modern plays do not elevate or do not purge pity and fear, and since they emphasize the forces that destroy man, they are not considered tragedies by many critics. Whether this judgment is accurate or whether any tragedy really provides a cathartic experience, one has to decide for himself.

Any response to tragedy, however, must be based on tolerance and understanding. If one applies rigid moral values to tragedy, he will not participate in the tragic experience. For instance, if one resents Othello because he killed his wife, he will miss the tragic moments of Othello's self-recognition and self-destruction. On the other hand, many students of tragedy argue that too much compassion will force one to accept any unhappy circumstances or results as tragic. They feel that a distinction must be made between what is pitiable and what is tragic.

Understatement is the deliberate underplaying of an emotion, thought, judgment, or situation. When emotion is involved, an author will sometimes employ understatement to imply that the emotion is too powerful or too vast to express. The lack of stress creates in the reader's mind an ironic difference between what the author actually says and what the circumstances would really allow him to say.

In Wordsworth's "Michael," the agonizing grief of Michael, who is disappointed in his only son, is characterized by the simple line "And never lifted up a single stone." In context this understated and negative action is effective, for the incomplete stone building which Michael and his son had started symbolizes the utter failure of the father's hopes.

The opposite of understatement is, of course, deliberate exaggeration for effect. This is frequently referred to as hyperbole.

SUGGESTIONS FOR ANALYZING LITERATURE

Throughout this book numerous ways to analyze literature have been discussed. The study aids in this appendix will bring many of these together by means of grouped questions which can be applied to any narrative (short story, novel, and drama) and to poetry. The questions should be used in conjunction with Chapter 1 and with the Glossary.

If used during the reading process, these questions can assist a student in comprehending what he reads. For this reason, the student should attempt to answer as many of the questions as possible. Even if he can answer some of them with a simple *yes* or *no*, he should not stop there: he must explain and develop his negative or affirmative answer if he is to evolve satisfactory material for his essay.

On the other hand, when the student begins to write his theme, he must concentrate only on those questions suitable to the purpose of his essay. Even though, when linked together, these questions provide a synthesis of many ways to analyze literature, they must be used in a limited sense for theme writing. A paper that attempts to answer every question would be a monstrosity — a conglomeration of comments thrown together without clear focus. Actually it is possible that a single question could provide enough insights and information for an interpretative essay.

SUGGESTIONS FOR ANALYZING FICTION[1]

Plot and Plot Structure

1) What are the main developments in the plot? Can you summarize the action?

2)   What is the point of view? Is it consistent? If not, why not? How is the point of view related to the structure of the plot — the way the material is held together?

3)   Can the narrative be divided into parts? What are they? How are they connected? How are parts which are not consecutive related to one another?

4)   Does the plot movement contain a climax? How does the author arrange events to build up to the climax? What is the purpose of details and events after the climax?

5)   Does the author use one character or a conflict between characters as the focal point of his structure?

6)   Has the author arranged the structure of his plot to achieve suspense?

7)   Does the author use techniques like motifs, symbols, contrast, or irony to help establish a unity of structure?

8)   Do the events occur logically and naturally, on the basis of cause and effect, or does the author contrive the events artificially in order to achieve an effect or purpose?

9)   Does the story provide a sense of totality? Do all the events and details contribute to a single effect, impression, illusion, or theme (or patterns of these)? Or is the structure intentionally loose and sprawling (for example, to accommodate stream of consciousness)?

Characterization

1)   What means or techniques does the author use to develop his characters? How is point of view related to characterization?

2)   What are the important traits of the main character or characters? Do the traits constitute a pattern of character? What details best support your interpretation of the character?

3)   What are the forces, internal and/or external, which motivate and shape the character's actions and personality? Are these forces due to a clash of wills or ideas? Are they related to the character's reactions to his environment, or are they related to his neuroses and psychoses (internal conflicts over which the character has little or no control)? Are the external forces affecting a person due to a concept of fate, or do they cause inner confusions and frustrations?

4)   Are the character's deeds and words believably motivated? Are they consistent? If not, is there any valid reason for inconsistent or unexpected conduct?

---

1. This article appeared originally in *Exercise Exchange*, December 1957, and is reprinted here, in a revised version, by permission of Holt, Rinehart and Winston, Inc.

5) If during the course of a story a character changes, is the change appropriate and well prepared for?

6) Is the character a realistic human being? Is he idealized too much? Is he a type (representative, but not individualized)? Is he a caricature?

Setting and Atmosphere

1) What is the basic setting of the story, and what atmosphere or mood radiates from it?

2) Does the setting change? What connection do the changes have with the structure of the plot?

3) Is the setting important in establishing conflict or in making an impact on the people in the narrative?

4) Would the story have been as meaningful if its action had occurred in another time and location?

5) Do the characters and ideas transcend the setting and become universal in a symbolical sense?

Style

1) Is the style straightforward or connotative and figurative?

2) How would you describe the author's vocabulary or choice of words?

3) How well does the author handle description and sense impressions?

4) Is economy of expression characteristic of the style? If not, why?

5) What are the main characteristics of the author's sentence patterns?

6) How does the author's use of dialog contribute to his style?

7) How does the author's tone affect his style? If there is a shift of tone, how does the change affect the style?

8) What adjectives (for example, graceful, verbose, lively, dull, terse, simple) best describe the author's style?

9) Has the author written in a style appropriate to his story, his characters, or his purpose? Or should he have used different levels of language, sentence patterns, etc., to achieve his aims?

10) Is the author's emphasis on how he writes more important than what he says, or is there a meaningful and artistic fusion of style and content?

Theme and Meaning

1)   Does the work emphasize a theme or a group of related themes—social, political, economic, psychological, moral and/or spiritual?

2)   Does the title of the work mirror the theme or give significant clues about it?

3)   Is the presentation of the theme direct or indirect? Didactic or subtle?

4)   What are the chief technical resources the author uses to shape his meaning or content? What insights into the meaning of the work has your study of plot structure, characterization, setting, and/or style provided?

5)   Has the author achieved a satisfactory fusion of form and content—a shaping of his ideas by technique?

SUGGESTIONS FOR ANALYZING POETRY

Literal Versus Figurative Meaning

1)   Can the poem be paraphrased on the literal level?

2)   Is there any evidence (such as key words, repetition of images, symbols, etc.) which leads you to suspect that the poem must be taken beyond paraphrase?

3)   Does the poet's tendency to compress his material create the possibility for multiple interpretations?

4)   Are there deliberate ambiguities which allow for multiple interpretation?

Imagery

1)   Is the poem free of images? Does direct language dominate the poem?

2)   Does the author primarily use purely descriptive images, those which appeal to the senses?

3)   Is the imagery based on association (the psychological process whereby you are led to link two elements)?

4)   Which of the following figures of speech (all of which involve association) are being used in the poem—simile, metaphor, symbol, allusion, personification? How do they function in the poem?

5)   Do the images fall into patterns related to the meaning? Do these patterns in effect become dominant symbols lifting the reader beyond the literal level?

Diction

1) What general term would you use to describe the author's choice of words—artificial and stilted, highly ornate, Latinate, archaic, abstract, conversational or colloquial, rhetorical, sentimental, intensely emotional, trite, etc.?

2) Does the author rely heavily on unusual words? Why?

3) Does he rely heavily on simple colloquial language? Why?

4) What words seem significant—connotative or suggestive of figurative meaning? How are these words related to their context?

5) Does the poet's desire to present musical effects (meter or rhyme) influence his choice of words? If this influence is heavy, is the quality of the poem marred?

6) Does the author's time or environment have anything to do with the language he uses? Do any of the words he uses have different meanings today?

7) Can you substitute words of your own for some used by the author? Which are better? Why? Does this experiment help you understand the difference between poetic diction and ordinary diction?

Musical Characteristics

1) Rhythm:

a) Can you determine a pattern of stress? Does the pattern fit any of the traditional patterns, such as iambic?

b) Does the pattern vary? If so, are these variations due to carelessness, or do they have purpose (in terms of meaning, emotional intensity, etc.)?

c) Is the pattern irregular enough to be called free verse?

d) What functions do pauses perform in the sound pattern?

e) Are there run-on lines? What effect do these have? How are syntax, syllabication, punctuation, and the lack of punctuation related to sound?

f) Does the meaning and/or purpose of the poem or of a given line or passage help you determine how it should be read (tone of voice, pitch, speed of delivery, etc.)?

g) If the music is entirely regular or even monotonous, is this quality due to a failure of the poet or to a purpose which is supported by the meaning of the poem?

2) Rhyme:
   a) Is there a rhyme scheme? Is it dictated by convention? Or is it original?
   b) What relevance does the rhyme scheme have to the music of the poem? Does it help or impede the sound pattern?
   c) Are there irregular rhymes? If so, why? Are they due to chronological changes in the pronunciation of words or to the poet's desire to pun?
   d) If there is no rhyme, is the author using a traditional pattern like blank verse, or does he have some other reason for avoiding rhyme?
   e) Is internal rhyme used? Why?
   f) Does rhyme or absence of rhyme contribute anything to your understanding of the poem?

3) Other musical devices:
   a) Does the poet use any of the following musical devices: alliteration, assonance, consonance, onomatopoeia, parallelism?
   b) What do these contribute to the mood and meaning of the poem?

Structure

1) If the poem can be classified as a sonnet, ode, elegy, etc., is its structure influenced by the conventions of the classification? If the poem deviates from the conventions, how is the structure affected?

2) What devices provide structural ties and arrangements for the poem? (See p. 14.)

3) What is the relationship of structural devices to the meaning of the poem?

4) Does the poet achieve a "totality of effect" – a unity of all poetic means?

Summary Questions

1) Which of the following purposes does the poem seem to have – to stress ideas offering insight into human nature and situations or into abstract ideas; to tell a story; to express an emotion; to create a mood or atmosphere; to describe some scene, thing, or person; to amuse; to satirize; or to accomplish any combination of these or any purpose not listed here?

2) What means does the author use to achieve his purpose? Could he have used other approaches?

3) Does the author successfully achieve his purpose?

4) What are the outstanding relationships in the poem between form (poetic technique) and content? Is the poem merely a technical display? Is it made unpoetic by a domination of ideas (content)?

THEME GRADING CHART

BRIEF DESCRIPTION

Theme Idea

T.I.1   You have no theme idea which binds or controls every-thing in the essay, or no statement of your theme idea emerges clearly enough. (See pp. 36-41 and 60-61.)

T.I.2   Because you have failed to limit your theme idea, you are unable to develop a precise pattern of organization, and/or you are forced to offer little beyond vague and sweeping generalizations. (See pp. 36-40 and 43-44.)

T.I.3   The theme idea is so limited that you are unable to offer any complex development of your subject. (See pp. 37 and 52-55.)

T.I.4   Your theme idea is so poorly or imprecisely stated that you have not established adequate guidelines for your-self and for your readers. (See pp. 37 and 83-87.)

T.I.5   Your theme idea must be stated more fully so that you can carefully define your key terms or prepare for the complex content of your essay. The absence of defi-nitions may have caused you to be vague or to lose focus on your purpose. (See pp. 37-38, 40, and 52-55.)

T.I.6   You have allowed the full development of your theme idea in your introduction to dominate your essay; as a result, you have not sufficiently developed the points made in your statement of purpose. (See pp. 40 and 69-71.)

T.I.7   You should state the theme idea early in your composition so that your readers may know what your purpose is and so that you may have a master plan to follow. (See pp. 40-41.)

Solidity of Content

C.1   You offer little more than a series of disconnected generalizations. (See pp. 43-44.)

C.2   The generalization in your theme idea is not advanced or developed because of repetition or the introduction of other big generalizations. (See p. 44.)

C.3   The paragraph is undernourished; the topic sentence should be developed by details and more complex analysis. (See p. 45.)

C.4   The generalization referred to by the symbol needs to be developed by means of specific details and interpretation. (See pp. 45-46.)

C.5   Since your essay is essentially a plot summary or paraphrase, you have neglected analysis of the story, poem, or play. (See pp. 3-5.)

C.6   Your essay consists of an ineffective mixture of summary and analysis. Hence your interpretation is dominated and perhaps buried by plot details. (See pp. 46-47.)

C.7   In moving from one paragraph to the next, use an idea rather than a plot detail to introduce the new paragraph. (See pp. 47-48.)

C.8   Avoid a scissors and paste approach. (See pp. 48-49.)

C.9   Do not distort interpretation by unconscious slanting, by omitting details, or by taking them out of context to prove your point. (See pp. 49-51.)

C.10   Do not interpret details at such a literal level that the work is oversimplified. (See pp. 51-52.)

C.11   Your theme is correctly written and adequately organized, but the analysis is superficial. (See pp. 52-55.)

C.12   You should do more than label and list details. Show how and why they relate to the point you claim they support. (See pp. 55-56.)

C.13   Follow the recommended three-step procedure. (See pp. 55-58.)

Organization

O.1   You do not have a clear focus on your theme idea. As a result this part of the paper is seemingly off the subject, or its relevance to the theme idea is not made clear enough. (See pp. 60-61.)

O.2   A transition is needed to eliminate a thought gap, to link sentences within a paragraph, to join paragraphs, or to make relevance of details and ideas clear. (See pp. 61-65.)

O.3   The arrangement of the major parts of your theme is not clear; the theme does not have a logical outline. For example, there may be a lack of climactic order. (See pp. 65-66.)

O.4   Although your main divisions are clearly arranged, you have not provided an orderly progression of parts within a major section. A paragraph should be placed with other material on the same aspect of your theme idea. (See pp. 66-67.)

O.5   Because the paragraph lacks unity and/or coherence, the organization of the theme momentarily breaks down. (See pp. 67-68.)

O.6   By making a running commentary on the literary work, you have made the organization of your paper confusing and ineffective. (See pp. 68-69.)

O.7   The organization lacks proper balance (proportion) in that you have devoted much more attention to one major part than to other sections of your paper. You may have given a minor point undue prominence. (See pp. 69-71.)

O.8   Your theme of comparison needs a more logical and consistent pattern of organization. (See pp. 78-82.)

Style

S.1   The meaning does not emerge because of garbled sentence structure or inexact choice of words. (See pp. 83-85.)

S.2   Wordiness impedes the movement of your discussion. (See pp. 85-86.)

S.3   Avoid jargon. (See pp. 86-87.)

S.4   Because the quotation is poorly integrated, the fluency of your essay is momentarily impeded. (See pp. 87-89.)

Nathaniel Hawthorne

THE AMBITIOUS GUEST

One September night a family had gathered round their hearth, and piled it high with the driftwood of mountain streams, the dry cones of the pine, and the splintered ruins of great trees that had come crashing down the precipice. Up the chimney roared the fire, and brightened the room with its broad blaze. The faces of the father and mother had a sober gladness; the children laughed; the eldest daughter was the image of Happiness at seventeen; and the aged grandmother, who sat knitting in the warmest place, was the image of Happiness grown old. They had found the "herb, heart's-ease," in the bleakest spot of all New England. This family were situated in the Notch of the White Hills, where the wind was sharp throughout the year, and pitilessly cold in the winter, — giving their cottage all its fresh inclemency before it descended on the valley of the Saco. They dwelt in a cold spot and a dangerous one; for a mountain towered above their heads, so steep, that the stones would often rumble down its sides and startle them at midnight.

The daughter had just uttered some simple jest that filled them all with mirth, when the wind came through the Notch and seemed to pause before their cottage — rattling the door, with a sound of wailing and lamentation, before it passed into the valley. For a moment it saddened them, though there was nothing unusual in the tones. But the family were glad again when they perceived that the latch was lifted by some traveller, whose footsteps had been unheard amid the dreary blast which heralded his approach, and wailed as he was entering, and went moaning away from the door.

Though they dwelt in such a solitude, these people held

daily converse with the world. The romantic pass of the Notch is a great artery, through which the lifeblood of internal commerce is continually throbbing between Maine, on one side, and the Green Mountains and the shores of the St. Lawrence, on the other. The stage-coach always drew up before the door of the cottage. The wayfarer, with no companion but his staff, paused here to exchange a word, that the sense of loneliness might not utterly overcome him ere he could pass through the cleft of the mountain, or reach the first house in the valley. And here the teamster, on his way to Portland market, would put up for the night; and, if a bachelor, might sit an hour beyond the usual bedtime, and steal a kiss from the mountain maid at parting. It was one of those primitive taverns where the traveller pays only for food and lodging, but meets with a homely kindness beyond all price. When the footsteps were heard, therefore, between the outer door and the inner one, the whole family rose up, grandmother, children, and all, as if about to welcome some one who belonged to them, and whose fate was linked with theirs.

The door was opened by a young man. His face at first wore the melancholy expression, almost despondency, of one who travels a wild and bleak road, at nightfall and alone, but soon brightened up when he saw the kindly warmth of his reception. He felt his heart spring forward to meet them all, from the old woman, who wiped a chair with her apron, to the little child that held out its arms to him. One glance and smile placed the stranger on a footing of innocent familiarity with the eldest daughter.

"Ah, this fire is the right thing!" cried he; "especially when there is such a pleasant circle round it. I am quite benumbed; for the Notch is just like the pipe of a great pair of bellows; it has blown a terrible blast in my face all the way from Bartlett."

"Then you are going towards Vermont?" said the master of the house, as he helped to take a light knapsack off the young man's shoulders.

"Yes; to Burlington, and far enough beyond," replied he. "I meant to have been at Ethan Crawford's to-night; but a pedestrian lingers along such a road as this. It is no matter; for, when I saw this good fire, and all your cheerful faces, I felt as if you had kindled it on purpose for me, and were waiting my arrival. So I shall sit down among you, and make myself at home."

The frank-hearted stranger had just drawn his chair to the fire when something like a heavy footstep was heard without, rushing down the steep side of the mountain, as with long and rapid strides, and taking such a leap in passing the cottage as to strike the opposite precipice. The family held their breath, because they knew the sound, and their guest held his by instinct.

"The old mountain has thrown a stone at us, for fear we should forget him," said the landlord, recovering himself. "He sometimes nods his head and threatens to come down; but we are old neighbors, and agree together pretty well upon the whole. Besides we have a sure place of refuge hard by if he should be coming in good earnest."

Let us now suppose the stranger to have finished his supper of bear's meat; and, by his natural felicity of manner, to have placed himself on a footing of kindness with the whole family, so that they talked as freely together as if he belonged to their mountain brood. He was of a proud, yet gentle spirit—haughty and reserved among the rich and great; but ever ready to stoop his head to the lowly cottage door, and be like a brother or a son at the poor man's fireside. In the household of the Notch he found warmth and simplicity of feeling, the pervading intelligence of New England, and a poetry of native growth, which they had gathered when they little thought of it from the mountain peaks and chasms, and at the very threshold of their romantic and dangerous abode. He had travelled far and alone; his whole life, indeed, had been a solitary path; for, with the lofty caution of his nature, he had kept himself apart from those who might otherwise have been his companions. The family, too, though so kind and hospitable, had that consciousness of unity among themselves, and separation from the world at large, which, in every domestic circle, should still keep a holy place where no stranger may intrude. But this evening a prophetic sympathy impelled the refined and educated youth to pour out his heart before the simple mountaineers, and constrained them to answer him with the same free confidence. And thus it should have been. Is not the kindred of a common fate a closer tie than that of birth?

The secret of the young man's character was a high and abstracted ambition. He could have borne to live an undistinguished life, but not to be forgotten in the grave. Yearning desire had been transformed to hope; and hope, long cherished, had become like certainty, that, obscurely as he journeyed now, a glory was to beam on all his pathway,—though not, perhaps, while he was treading it. But when posterity should gaze back into the gloom of what was now the present, they would trace the brightness of his footsteps, brightening as meaner glories faded, and confess that a gifted one had passed from his cradle to his tomb with none to recognize him.

"As yet," cried the stranger—his cheek glowing and his eye flashing with enthusiasm—"as yet, I have done nothing. Were I to vanish from the earth to-morrow, none would know so much of me as you: that a nameless youth came up at nightfall from the valley of the Saco, and opened his heart to you in the evening, and passed through the Notch by sunrise, and was seen no more. Not a soul would ask, 'Who was he? Whither did the wanderer go?' But I cannot die till I have achieved my destiny. Then, let Death come! I shall have built my monument!"

There was a continual flow of natural emotion, gushing forth amid abstracted reverie, which enabled the family to understand this young man's sentiments, though so foreign from their own. With quick sensibility of the ludicrous, he blushed at the ardor into which he had been betrayed.

"You laugh at me," said he, taking the eldest daughter's hand, and laughing himself. "You think my ambition as nonsensical as if I were to freeze myself to death on the top of Mount Washington, only that people might spy at me from the country round about. And, truly, that would be a noble pedestal for a man's statue!"

"It is better to sit here by this fire," answered the girl, blushing, "and be comfortable and contented, though nobody thinks about us."

"I suppose," said her father, after a fit of musing, "there is something natural in what the young man says; and if my mind had been turned that way, I might have felt just the same. It is strange, wife, how his talk has set my head running on things that are pretty certain never to come to pass."

"Perhaps they may," observed the wife. "Is the man thinking what he will do when he is a widower?"

"No, no!" cried he, repelling the idea with reproachful kindness. "When I think of your death, Esther, I think of mine, too. But I was wishing we had a good farm in Bartlett, or Bethlehem, or Littleton, or some other township round the White Mountains; but not where they could tumble on our heads. I should want to stand well with my neighbors and be called Squire, and sent to General Court for a term or two; for a plain, honest man may do as much good there as a lawyer. And when I should be grown quite an old man, and you an old woman, so as not to be long apart, I might die happy enough in my bed, and leave you all crying around me. A slate gravestone would suit me as well as a marble one—with just my name and age, and a verse of a hymn, and something to let people know that I lived an honest man and died a Christian."

"There now!" exclaimed the stranger; "it is our nature to desire a monument, be it slate or marble, or a pillar of granite, or a glorious memory in the universal heart of man."

"We're in a strange way, to-night," said the wife, with tears in her eyes. "They say it's a sign of something, when folks' minds go a wandering so. Hark to the children!"

They listened accordingly. The younger children had been put to bed in another room, but with an open door between, so that they could be heard talking busily among themselves. One and all seemed to have caught the infection from the fireside circle, and were outvying each other in wild wishes, and childish projects of what they would do when they came to be men and women. At length a little boy, instead of addressing his brothers and sisters, called out to his mother.

"I'll tell you what I wish, mother," cried he. "I want you and father and grandma'm, and all of us, and the stranger too, to start right away, and go and take a drink out of the basin of the Flume!"

Nobody could help laughing at the child's notion of leaving a warm bed, and dragging them from a cheerful fire, to visit the basin of the Flume, — a brook, which tumbles over the precipice, deep within the Notch. The boy had hardly spoken when a wagon rattled along the road, and stopped a moment before the door. It appeared to contain two or three men, who were cheering their hearts with the rough chorus of a song, which resounded, in broken notes, between the cliffs, while the singers hesitated whether to continue their journey or put up here for the night.

"Father," said the girl, "they are calling you by name."

But the good man doubted whether they had really called him, and was unwilling to show himself too solicitous of gain by inviting people to patronize his house. He therefore did not hurry to the door; and the lash being soon applied, the travellers plunged into the Notch, still singing and laughing, though their music and mirth came back drearily from the heart of the mountain.

"There, mother!" cried the boy, again. "They'd have given us a ride to the Flume."

Again they laughed at the child's pertinacious fancy for a night ramble. But it happened that a light cloud passed over the daughter's spirit; she looked gravely into the fire, and drew a breath that was almost a sigh. It forced its way, in spite of a little struggle to repress it. Then starting and blushing, she looked quickly round the circle, as if they had caught a glimpse into her bosom. The stranger asked what she had been thinking of.

"Nothing," answered she, with a downcast smile. "Only I felt lonesome just then."

"Oh, I have always had a gift of feeling what is in other people's hearts," said he, half seriously. "Shall I tell the secrets of yours? For I know what to think when a young girl shivers by a warm hearth, and complains of lonesomeness at her mother's side. Shall I put these feelings into words?"

"They would not be a girl's feelings any longer if they could be put into words," replied the mountain nymph, laughing, but avoiding his eye.

All this was said apart. Perhaps a germ of love was springing in their hearts, so pure that it might blossom in Paradise, since it could not be matured on earth; for women worship such gentle dignity as his; and the proud, contemplative, yet kindly soul is oftenest captivated by simplicity like hers. But while they spoke softly, and he was watching the happy sadness, the lightsome shadows, the shy yearnings of a maiden's nature, the wind through the Notch took a deeper and drearier sound. It seemed, as the fanciful stranger said, like the choral strain of the spirits of the blast, who in old Indian times had their dwelling among these mountains, and made their heights and recesses a sacred region. There was a wail along the road, as if a funeral were passing. To chase away the gloom, the family threw pine branches on their fire, till the dry leaves crackled and the flame arose, discovering once again a scene of peace and humble happiness. The light hovered about them fondly, and caressed them all. There were the little faces of the children, peeping from their bed apart, and here the father's frame of strength, the mother's subdued and careful mien, the high-browed youth, the budding girl, and the good old grandam, still knitting in the warmest place. The aged woman looked up from her task, and, with fingers ever busy, was the next to speak.

"Old folks have their notions," said she, "as well as young ones. You've been wishing and planning; and letting your heads run on one thing and another, till you've set my mind a wandering too. Now what should an old woman wish for, when she can go but a step or two before she comes to her grave? Children, it will haunt me night and day till I tell you."

"What is it, mother?" cried the husband and wife at once.

Then the old woman, with an air of mystery which drew the circle closer round the fire, informed them that she had provided her grave-clothes some years before, — a nice linen shroud, a cap with a muslin ruff, and everything of a finer sort than she had worn since her wedding day. But this evening an old superstition had strangely recurred to her. It used to be said, in her younger days, that if anything were amiss with a corpse, if only the ruff were not smooth, or the cap did not set right, the corpse in the coffin and beneath the clods would strive to put up its cold hands and arrange it. The bare thought made her nervous.

"Don't talk so, grandmother!" said the girl, shuddering.

"Now," — continued the old woman, with singular earnestness, yet smiling strangely at her own folly, — "I want one of you, my children — when your mother is dressed and in the coffin — I want one of you to hold a looking-glass over my face. Who knows but I may take a glimpse at myself, and see whether all's right?"

"Old and young, we dream of graves and monuments," murmured the stranger youth. "I wonder how mariners feel when the ship is sinking, and they, unknown and undistinguished, are to be buried together in the ocean — that wide and nameless sepulchre?"

For a moment, the old woman's ghastly conception so engrossed the minds of her hearers that a sound abroad in the night, rising like the roar of a blast, had grown broad, deep, and terrible, before the fated group were conscious of it. The house and all within it trembled; the foundations of the earth seemed to be shaken, as if this awful sound were the peal of the last trump. Young and old exchanged one wild glance, and remained an instant, pale, affrighted, without utterance, or power to move. Then the same shriek burst simultaneously from all their lips.

"The Slide! The Slide!"

The simplest words must intimate, but not portray, the unutterable horror of the catastrophe. The victims rushed from their cottage, and sought refuge in what they deemed a safer spot — where, in contemplation of such an emergency, a sort of barrier had been reared. Alas! they had quitted their security, and fled right into the pathway of destruction. Down came the whole side of the mountain, in a cataract of ruin. Just before it reached the house, the stream broke into two branches — shivered not a window there, but overwhelmed the whole vicinity, blocked up the road, and annihilated everything in its dreadful course. Long ere the thunder of the great Slide had ceased to roar among the mountains, the mortal agony had been endured, and the victims were at peace. Their bodies were never found.

The next morning, the light smoke was seen stealing from

the cottage chimney up the mountain side. Within, the fire was yet smouldering on the hearth, and the chairs in a circle round it, as if the inhabitants had but gone forth to view the devastation of the Slide, and would shortly return, to thank Heaven for their miraculous escape. All had left separate tokens, by which those who had known the family were made to shed a tear for each. Who has not heard their name? The story has been told far and wide, and will forever be a legend of these mountains. Poets have sung their fate.

There were circumstances which led some to suppose that a stranger had been received into the cottage on this awful night, and had shared the catastrophe of all its inmates. Others denied that there were sufficient grounds for such a conjecture. Woe for the high-souled youth, with his dream of Earthly Immortality! His name and person utterly unknown; his history, his way of life, his plans, a mystery never to be solved, his death and his existence equally a doubt! Whose was the agony of that death moment?

Katherine Anne Porter

FLOWERING JUDAS[1]

Braggioni sits heaped upon the edge of a straightbacked chair much too small for him, and sings to Laura in a furry, mournful voice. Laura has begun to find reasons for avoiding her own house until the latest possible moment, for Braggioni is there almost every night. No matter how late she is, he will be sitting there with a surly, waiting expression, pulling at his kinky yellow hair, thumbing the strings of his guitar, snarling a tune under his breath. Lupe the Indian maid meets Laura at the door, and says with a flicker of a glance toward the upper room, "He waits."

Laura wishes to lie down, she is tired of her hairpins and the feel of her long tight sleeves, but she says to him, "Have you a new song for me this evening?" If he says yes, she asks him to sing it. If he says no, she remembers his favorite one, and asks him to sing it again. Lupe brings her a cup of chocolate and a plate of rice, and Laura eats at the small table under the lamp, first inviting Braggioni, whose answer is always the same: "I have eaten, and besides, chocolate thickens the voice."

Laura says, "Sing, then," and Braggioni heaves himself into song. He scratches the guitar familiarly as though it were a pet animal, and sings passionately off key, taking the high notes in a prolonged painful squeal. Laura, who haunts the markets listening to the ballad singers, and stops every day to hear the blind boy playing his reed-flute in Sixteenth of September Street, listens to Braggioni with pitiless courtesy, because she dares not smile at his miserable performance. Nobody dares to smile

1. From *Flowering Judas and Other Stories*, copyright 1930, 1935, © 1958 by Katherine Anne Porter. Reprinted by permission of Harcourt, Brace & World, Inc.

at him. Braggioni is cruel to everyone, with a kind of specialized insolence, but he is so vain of his talents, and so sensitive to slights, it would require a cruelty and vanity greater than his own to lay a finger on the vast cureless wound of his self-esteem. It would require courage, too, for it is dangerous to offend him, and nobody has this courage.

Braggioni loves himself with such tenderness and amplitude and eternal charity that his followers — for he is a leader of men, a skilled revolutionist, and his skin has been punctured in honorable warfare — warm themselves in the reflected glow, and say to each other: "He has a real nobility, a love of humanity raised above mere personal affections." The excess of this self-love has flowed out, inconveniently for her, over Laura, who, with so many others, owes her comfortable situation and her salary to him. When he is in a very good humor, he tells her, "I am tempted to forgive you for being a *gringa. Gringita!*" and Laura, burning, imagines herself leaning forward suddenly, and with a sound back-handed slap wiping the suety smile from his face. If he notices her eyes at these moments he gives no sign.

She knows what Braggioni would offer her, and she must resist tenaciously without appearing to resist, and if she could avoid it she could not admit even to herself the slow drift of his intention. During these long evenings which have spoiled a long month for her, she sits in her deep chair with an open book on her knees, resting her eyes on the consoling rigidity of the printed page when the sight and sound of Braggioni singing threaten to identify themselves with all her remembered afflictions and to add their weight to her uneasy premonitions of the future. The gluttonous bulk of Braggioni has become a symbol of her many disillusions, for a revolutionist should be lean, animated by heroic faith, a vessel of abstract virtues. This is nonsense, she knows it now and is ashamed of it. Revolution must have leaders, and leadership is a career for energetic men. She is, her comrades tell her, full of romantic error, for what she defines as cynicism in them is merely "a developed sense of reality." She is almost too willing to say, "I am wrong, I suppose I don't really understand the principles," and afterward she makes a secret truce with herself, determined not to surrender her will to such expedient logic. But she cannot help feeling that she has been betrayed irreparably by the disunion between her way of living and her feeling of what life should be, and at times she is almost contented to rest in this sense of grievance as a private store of consolation. Sometimes she wishes to run away, but she stays.

Now she longs to fly out of this room, down the narrow stairs, and into the street where the houses lean together like conspirators under a single mottled lamp, and leave Braggioni singing to himself.

Instead she looks at Braggioni, frankly and clearly, like a good child who understands the rules of behavior. Her knees cling together under sound blue serge, and her round white collar is not purposely nun-like. She wears the uniform of an idea, and has renounced vanities. She was born Roman Catholic, and in spite of her fear of being seen by someone who might make a scandal of it, she slips now and again into some crumbling little church, kneels on the chilly stone, and says a Hail Mary on the gold rosary she bought in Tehuantepec. It is no good and she ends by examining the altar with its tinsel flowers and ragged brocades, and feels tender about the battered doll-shape of some male saint whose white, lace-trimmed drawers hang limply around his ankles below the hieratic dignity of his velvet robe. She has encased herself in a set of principles derived from her early training, leaving no detail of gesture or of personal taste untouched, and for this reason she will not wear lace made on machines. This is her private heresy, for in her special group the machine is sacred, and will be the salvation of the workers. She loves fine lace, and there is a tiny edge of fluted cobweb on this collar, which is one of twenty precisely alike, folded in blue tissue paper in the upper drawer of her clothes chest.

Braggioni catches her glance solidly as if he had been waiting for it, leans forward, balancing his paunch between his spread knees, and sings with tremendous emphasis, weighing his words. He has, the song relates, no father and no mother, nor even a friend to console him; lonely as a wave of the sea he comes and goes, lonely as a wave. His mouth opens round and yearns sideways, his balloon cheeks grow oily with the labor of song. He bulges marvelously in his expensive garments. Over his lavender collar, crushed upon a purple necktie, held by a diamond hoop: over his ammunition belt of tooled leather worked in silver, buckled cruelly around his gasping middle: over the tops of his glossy yellow shoes Braggioni swells with ominous ripeness, his mauve silk hose stretched taut, his ankles bound with the stout leather thongs of his shoes.

When he stretches his eyelids at Laura she notes again that his eyes are the true tawny yellow cat's eyes. He is rich, not in money, he tells her, but in power, and this power brings with it the blameless ownership of things, and the right to indulge

his love of small luxuries. "I have a taste for the elegant re-
finements," he said once, flourishing a yellow silk handkerchief
before her nose. "Smell that? It is Jockey Club, imported from
New York." Nonetheless he is wounded by life. He will say so
presently. "It is true everything turns to dust in the hand, to gall
on the tongue." He sighs and his leather belt creaks like a saddle
girth. "I am disappointed in everything as it comes. Everything."
He shakes his head. "You, poor thing, you will be disappointed
too. You are born for it. We are more alike than you realize in
some things. Wait and see. Some day you will remember what I
have told you, you will know that Braggioni was your friend."

Laura feels a slow chill, a purely physical sense of danger, a
warning in her blood that violence, mutilation, a shocking death,
wait for her with lessening patience. She has translated this fear
into something homely, immediate, and sometimes hesitates
before crossing the street. "My personal fate is nothing, except
as the testimony of a mental attitude," she reminds herself,
quoting from some forgotten philosophic primer, and is sensible
enough to add, "Anyhow, I shall not be killed by an automobile
if I can help it."

"It may be true I am as corrupt, in another way, as
Braggioni," she thinks in spite of herself, "as callous, as incomplete," and if this is so, any kind of death seems preferable. Still
she sits quietly, she does not run. Where could she go? Uninvited
she has promised herself to this place; she can no longer imagine
herself as living in another country, and there is no pleasure in
remembering her life before she came here.

Precisely what is the nature of this devotion, its true motives,
and what are its obligations? Laura cannot say. She spends part
of her days in Xochimilco, near by, teaching Indian children
to say in English, "The cat is on the mat." When she appears in
the classroom they crowd about her with smiles on their wise,
innocent, clay-colored faces, crying, "Good morning, my ticher!"
in immaculate voices, and they make of her desk a fresh garden
of flowers every day.

During her leisure she goes to union meetings and listens
to busy important voices quarreling over tactics, methods,
internal politics. She visits the prisoners of her own political
faith in their cells, where they entertain themselves with
counting cockroaches, repenting of their indiscretions, com-
posing their memoirs, writing out manifestoes and plans for their
comrades who are still walking about free, hands in pockets,
sniffing fresh air. Laura brings them food and cigarettes and a

little money, and she brings messages disguised in equivocal phrases from the men outside who dare not set foot in the prison for fear of disappearing into the cells kept empty for them. If the prisoners confuse night and day, and complain, "Dear little Laura, time doesn't pass in this infernal hole, and I won't know when it is time to sleep unless I have a reminder," she brings them their favorite narcotics, and says in a tone that does not wound them with pity, "Tonight will really be night for you," and though her Spanish amuses them, they find her comforting, useful. If they lose patience and all faith, and curse the slowness of their friends in coming to their rescue with money and influence, they trust her not to repeat everything, and if she inquires, "Where do you think we can find money, or influence?" they are certain to answer, "Well, there is Braggioni, why doesn't he do something?"

She smuggles letters from headquarters to men hiding from firing squads in back streets in mildewed houses, where they sit in tumbled beds and talk bitterly as if all Mexico were at their heels, when Laura knows positively they might appear at the band concert in the Alameda on Sunday morning, and no one would notice them. But Braggioni says, "Let them sweat a little. The next time they may be careful. It is very restful to have them out of the way for a while." She is not afraid to knock on any door in any street after midnight, and enter in the darkness, and say to one of these men who is really in danger: "They will be looking for you — seriously — tomorrow morning after six. Here is some money from Vicente. Go to Vera Cruz and wait."

She borrows money from the Roumanian agitator to give to his bitter enemy the Polish agitator. The favor of Braggioni is their disputed territory, and Braggioni holds the balance nicely, for he can use them both. The Polish agitator talks love to her over café tables, hoping to exploit what he believes is her secret sentimental preference for him, and he gives her misinformation which he begs her to repeat as the solemn truth to certain persons. The Roumanian is more adroit. He is generous with his money in all good causes, and lies to her with an air of ingenuous candor, as if he were her good friend and confidant. She never repeats anything they may say. Braggioni never asks questions. He has other ways to discover all that he wishes to know about them.

Nobody touches her, but all praise her gray eyes, and the soft, round under lip which promises gaiety, yet is always grave, nearly always firmly closed: and they cannot understand why she is in Mexico. She walks back and forth on her errands, with puzzled eyebrows, carrying her little folder of drawings and music and school papers. No dancer dances more beautifully than Laura walks, and she inspires some amusing, unexpected ardors, which cause little gossip, because nothing comes of them. A young captain who had been a soldier in Zapata's army attempted, during a horseback ride near Cuernavaca, to express his desire for her with the noble simplicity befitting a rude folk-hero: but gently, because he was gentle. This gentleness was his defeat, for when he alighted, and removed her foot from the stirrup, and essayed to draw her down into his arms, her horse, ordinarily a tame one, shied fiercely, reared and plunged away. The young hero's horse careered blindly after his stable-mate, and the hero did not return to the hotel until rather late that evening. At breakfast he came to her table in full charro dress, gray buckskin jacket and trousers with strings of silver buttons down the leg, and he was in a humorous, careless mood. "May I sit with you?" and "You are a wonderful rider. I was terrified that you might be thrown and dragged. I should never have forgiven myself. But I cannot admire you enough for your riding!"

"I learned to ride in Arizona," said Laura.

"If you will ride with me again this morning, I promise you a horse that will not shy with you," he said. But Laura remembered that she must return to Mexico City at noon.

Next morning the children made a celebration and spent their playtime writing on the blackboard, "We lov ar ticher," and with tinted chalks they drew wreaths of flowers around the words. The young hero wrote her a letter: "I am a very foolish, wasteful, impulsive man. I should have first said I love you, and then you would not have run away. But you shall see me again." Laura thought, "I must send him a box of colored crayons," but she was trying to forgive herself for having spurred her horse at the wrong moment.

A brown, shock-haired youth came and stood in her patio one night and sang like a lost soul for two hours, but Laura could think of nothing to do about it. The moonlight spread a wash of gauzy silver over the clear spaces of the garden, and the shadows were cobalt blue. The scarlet blossoms of the Judas tree were dull purple, and the names of the colors repeated themselves automatically in her mind, while she watched not the boy, but his shadow, fallen like a dark garment across the fountain rim, trailing in the water. Lupe came silently and whispered expert counsel in her ear: "If you will throw him one little flower, he

will sing another song or two and go away." Laura threw the
flower, and he sang a last song and went away with the flower
tucked in the band of his hat. Lupe said, "He is one of the organ-
izers of the Typographers Union, and before that he sold corridos
in the Merced market, and before that, he came from Guanajuato,
where I was born. I would not trust any man, but I trust least
those from Guanajuato."

She did not tell Laura that he would be back again the next
night, and the next, nor that he would follow her at a certain
fixed distance around the Merced market, through the Zócolo,
up Francisco I. Madero Avenue, and so along the Paseo de la
Reforma to Chapultepec Park, and into the Philosopher's Foot-
path, still with that flower withering in his hat, and an indivisi-
ble attention in his eyes.

Now Laura is accustomed to him, it means nothing except
that he is nineteen years old and is observing a convention with
all propriety, as though it were founded on a law of nature,
which in the end it might well prove to be. He is beginning
to write poems which he prints on a wooden press, and he leaves
them stuck like handbills in her door. She is pleasantly disturbed
by the abstract, unhurried watchfulness of his black eyes which
will in time turn easily towards another object. She tells herself
that throwing the flower was a mistake, for she is twenty-two
years old and knows better; but she refuses to regret it, and
persuades herself that her negation of all external events as
they occur is a sign that she is gradually perfecting herself
in the stoicism she strives to cultivate against that disaster she
fears, though she cannot name it.

She is not at home in the world. Every day she teaches
children who remain strangers to her, though she loves their
tender round hands and their charming opportunist savagery.
She knocks at unfamiliar doors not knowing whether a friend or
a stranger shall answer, and even if a known face emerges from
the sour gloom of that unknown interior, still it is the face of a
stranger. No matter what this stranger says to her, nor what
her message to him, the very cells of her flesh reject knowledge
and kinship in one monotonous word. No. No. No. She draws her
strength from this one holy talismanic word which does not
suffer her to be led into evil. Denying everything, she may walk
anywhere in safety, she looks at everything without amazement.

No, repeats this firm unchanging voice of her blood; and she
looks at Braggioni without amazement. He is a great man, he
wishes to impress this simple girl who covers her great round

breasts with thick dark cloth, and who hides long, invaluably beautiful legs under a heavy skirt. She is almost thin except for the incomprehensible fullness of her breasts, like a nursing mother's, and Braggioni, who considers himself a judge of women, speculates again on the puzzle of her notorious virginity, and takes the liberty of speech which she permits without a sign of modesty, indeed, without any sort of sign, which is disconcerting.

"You think you are so cold, *gringita!* Wait and see. You will surprise yourself some day! May I be there to advise you!" He stretches his eyelids at her, and his ill-humored cat's eyes waver in a separate glance for the two points of light marking the opposite ends of a smoothly drawn path between the swollen curve of her breasts. He is not put off by that blue serge, nor by her resolutely fixed gaze. There is all the time in the world. His cheeks are bellying with the wind of song. "O girl with the dark eyes," he sings, and reconsiders. "But yours are not dark. I can change all that. O girl with the green eyes, you have stolen my heart away!" then his mind wanders to the song, and Laura feels the weight of his attention being shifted elsewhere. Singing thus, he seems harmless, he is quite harmless, there is nothing to do but sit patiently and say "No," when the moment comes. She draws a full breath, and her mind wanders also, but not far. She dares not wander too far.

Not for nothing has Braggioni taken pains to be a good revolutionist and a professional lover of humanity. He will never die of it. He has the malice, the cleverness, the wickedness, the sharpness of wit, the hardness of heart, stipulated for loving the world profitably. *He will never die of it.* He will live to see himself kicked out from his feeding trough by other hungry world-saviours. Traditionally he must sing in spite of his life which drives him to bloodshed, he tells Laura, for his father was a Tuscany peasant who drifted to Yucatan and married a Maya woman: a woman of race, an aristocrat. They gave him the love and knowledge of music, thus: and under the rip of his thumbnail, the strings of the instrument complain like exposed nerves.

Once he was called Delgadito by all the girls and married women who ran after him; he was so scrawny all his bones showed under his thin cotton clothing, and he could squeeze his emptiness to the very backbone with his two hands. He was a poet and the revolution was only a dream then; too many women loved him and sapped away his youth, and he could never find enough to eat anywhere, anywhere! Now he is a leader of men, crafty men who whisper in his ear, hungry men who wait for hours outside his office for a word with him, emaciated men with wild faces who waylay him at the street gate with a timid, "Comrade, let me tell you..." and they blow the foul breath from their empty stomachs in his face.

He is always sympathetic. He gives them handfuls of small coins from his own pocket, he promises them work, there will be demonstrations, they must join the unions and attend the meetings, above all they must be on the watch for spies. They are closer to him than his own brothers, without them he can do nothing—until tomorrow, comrade!

Until tomorrow. "They are stupid, they are lazy, they are treacherous, they would cut my throat for nothing," he says to Laura. He has good food and abundant drink, he hires an automobile and drives in the Paseo on Sunday morning, and enjoys plenty of sleep in a soft bed beside a wife who dares not disturb him, and he sits pampering his bones in easy billows of fat, singing to Laura, who knows and thinks these things about him. When he was fifteen, he tried to drown himself because he loved a girl, his first love, and she laughed at him. "A thousand women have paid for that," and his tight little mouth turns down at the corners. Now he perfumes his hair with Jockey Club, and confides to Laura: "One woman is really as good as another for me, in the dark. I prefer them all."

His wife organizes unions among the girls in the cigarette factories, and walks in picket lines, and even speaks at meetings in the evening. But she cannot be brought to acknowledge the benefits of true liberty. "I tell her I must have my freedom, net. She does not understand my point of view." Laura has heard this many times. Braggioni scratches the guitar and meditates. "She is an instinctively virtuous woman, pure gold, no doubt of that. If she were not, I should lock her up, and she knows it."

His wife, who works so hard for the good of the factory girls, employs part of her leisure lying on the floor weeping because there are so many women in the world, and only one husband for her, and she never knows where nor when to look for him. He told her: "Unless you can learn to cry when I am not here, I must go away for good." That day he went away and took a room at the Hotel Madrid.

It is this month of separation for the sake of higher principles that has been spoiled not only for Mrs. Braggioni, whose sense of reality is beyond criticism, but for Laura, who feels herself bogged in a nightmare. Tonight Laura envies Mrs. Braggioni, who is alone, and free to weep as much as she pleases about a

concrete wrong. Laura has just come from a visit to the prison,
and she is waiting for tomorrow with a bitter anxiety as if
tomorrow may not come, but time may be caught immovably in
this hour, with herself transfixed, Braggioni singing on forever,
and Eugenio's body not yet discovered by the guard.

Braggioni says: "Are you going to sleep?" Almost before she
can shake her head, he begins telling her about the May-day
disturbances coming on in Morelia, for the Catholics hold a
festival in honor of the Blessed Virgin, and the Socialists celebrate their martyrs on that day. "There will be two independent
processions, starting from either end of town, and they will march
until they meet, and the rest depends . . ." He asks her to oil and
load his pistols. Standing up, he unbuckles his ammunition belt,
and spreads it laden across her knees. Laura sits with the shells
slipping through the cleaning cloth dipped in oil, and he says
again he cannot understand why she works so hard for the
revolutionary idea unless she loves some man who is in it. "Are
you not in love with someone?" "No," says Laura. "And no one
is in love with you?" "No." "Then it is your own fault. No woman
need go begging. Why, what is the matter with you? The legless
beggar woman in the Alameda has a perfectly faithful lover. Did
you know that?"

Laura peers down the pistol barrel and says nothing, but a
long, slow faintness rises and subsides in her; Braggioni curves
his swollen fingers around the throat of the guitar and softly
smothers the music out of it, and when she hears him again he
seems to have forgotten her, and is speaking in the hypnotic
voice he uses when talking in small rooms to a listening, close-
gathered crowd. Some day this world, now seemingly so composed
and eternal,. to the edges of every sea shall be merely a tangle
of gaping trenches, of crashing walls and broken bodies. Everything must be torn from its accustomed place where it has rotted
for centuries, hurled skyward and distributed, cast down again
clean as rain, without separate identity. Nothing shall survive
that the stiffened hands of poverty have created for the rich and
no one shall be left alive except the elect spirits destined to
procreate a new world cleansed of cruelty and injustice, ruled by
benevolent anarchy: "Pistols are good, I love them, cannon are
even better, but in the end I pin my faith to good dynamite," he
concludes, and strokes the pistol lying in her hands. "Once I
dreamed of destroying this city, in case it offered resistance to
General Ortíz, but it fell into his hands like an overripe pear."

He is made restless by his own words, rises and stands

waiting. Laura holds up the belt to him: "Put that on, and go kill somebody in Morelia, and you will be happier," she says softly. The presence of death in the room makes her bold. "Today, I found Eugenio going into a stupor. He refused to allow me to call the prison doctor. He had taken all the tablets I brought him yesterday. He said he took them because he was bored."

"He is a fool, and his death is his own business," says Braggioni, fastening his belt carefully.

"I told him if he had waited only a little while longer, you would have got him set free," says Laura. "He said he did not want to wait."

"He is a fool and we are well rid of him," says Braggioni, reaching for his hat.

He goes away. Laura knows his mood has changed, she will not see him any more for a while. He will send word when he needs her to go on errands into strange streets, to speak to the strange faces that will apppear, like clay masks with the power of human speech, to mutter their thanks to Braggioni for his help. Now she is free, and she thinks, I must run while there is time. But she does not go.

Braggioni enters his own house where for a month his wife has spent many hours every night weeping and tangling her hair upon her pillow. She is weeping now, and she weeps more at the sight of him, the cause of all her sorrows. He looks about the room. Nothing is changed, the smells are good and familiar, he is well acquainted with the woman who comes toward him with no reproach except grief on her face. He says to her tenderly: "You are so good, please don't cry any more, you dear good creature." She says, "Are you tired, my angel? Sit here and I will wash your feet." She brings a bowl of water, and kneeling, unlaces his shoes, and when from her knees she raises her sad eyes under her blackened lids, he is sorry for everything, and bursts into tears. "Ah, yes, I am hungry, I am tired, let us eat something together," he says, between sobs. His wife leans her head on his arm and says, "Forgive me!" and this time he is re- freshed by the solemn, endless rain of her tears.

Laura takes off her serge dress and puts on a white linen nightgown and goes to bed. She turns her head a little to one side, and lying still, reminds herself that it is time to sleep. Numbers tick in her brain like little clocks, soundless doors close of themselves around her. If you would sleep, you must not remember anything, the children will say tomorrow, good morning, my teacher, the poor prisoners who come every day bringing flowers to their jailor. 1-2-3-4-5 it is monstrous to confuse love with revolution, night with day, life with death — ah, Eugenio!

The tolling of the midnight bell is a signal, but what does it mean? Get up, Laura, and follow me: come out of your sleep, out of your bed, out of this strange house. What are you doing in this house? Without a word, without fear she rose and reached for Eugenio's hand, but he eluded her with a sharp, sly smile and drifted away. This is not all, you shall see — Murderer, he said, follow me, I will show you a new country, but it is far away and we must hurry. No, said Laura, not unless you take my hand, no; and she clung first to the stair rail, and then to the topmost branch of the Judas tree that bent down slowly and set her upon the earth, and then to the rocky ledge of a cliff, and then to the jagged wave of a sea that was not water but a desert of crumbling stone. Where are you taking me, she asked in wonder but without fear. To death, and it is a long way off, and we must hurry, said Eugenio. No, said Laura, not unless you take my hand. Then eat these flowers, poor prisoner, said Eugenio in a voice of pity, take and eat: and from the Judas tree he stripped the warm bleeding flowers, and held them to her lips. She saw that his hand was fleshless, a cluster of small white petrified branches, and his eye sockets were without light, but she ate the flowers greedily for they satisfied both hunger and thirst. Murderer! said Eugenio, and Cannibal! This is my body and my blood. Laura cried No! and at the sound of her own voice, she awoke trembling, and was afraid to sleep again.

Eudora Welty

OLD MR. MARBLEHALL[1]

Old Mr. Marblehall never did anything, never got married until he was sixty. You can see him out taking a walk. Watch and you'll see how preciously old people come to think they are made—the way they walk, like conspirators, bent over a little, filled with protection. They stand long on the corners but more impatiently than anyone, as if they expected traffic to take notice of them, rear up the horses and throw on the brakes, so they can go where they want to go. That's Mr. Marblehall. He has short white bangs, and a bit of snapdragon in his lapel. He walks with a big polished stick, a present. That's what people think of him. Everybody says to his face, "So well preserved!" Behind his back they say cheerfully, "One foot in the grave." He has on his thick, beautiful, glowing coat—tweed, but he looks as gratified as an animal in its own tingling fur. You see, even in summer he wears it, because he is cold all the time. He looks quaintly secretive and prepared for anything, out walking very luxuriously on Catherine Street.

His wife, back at home in the parlor standing up to think, is a large, elongated old woman with electric-looking hair and curly lips. She has spent her life trying to escape from the parlorlike jaws of self-consciousness. Her late marriage has set in upon her nerves like a retriever nosing and puffing through old dead leaves out in the woods. When she walks around the room she looks remote and nebulous, out on the fringe of habitation, and rather as if she must have been cruelly trained—otherwise she couldn't

1. From *A Curtain of Green and Other Stories,* copyright 1938 by Eudora Welty. Reprinted by permission of Harcourt, Brace & World, Inc.

do actual, immediate things, like answering the telephone or putting on a hat. But she has gone further than you'd think: into club work. Surrounded by other more suitably exclaiming women, she belongs to the Daughters of the American Revolution and the United Daughters of the Confederacy, attending teas. Her long, disquieted figure towering in the candlelight of other women's houses looks like something accidental. Any occasion, and she dresses her hair like a unicorn horn. She even sings, and is requested to sing. She even writes some of the songs she sings ("O Trees in the Evening"). She has a voice that dizzies other ladies like an organ note, and amuses men like a halloo down the well. It's full of a hollow wind and echo, winding out through the wavery hope of her mouth. Do people know of her perpetual amazement? Back in safety she wonders, her untidy head trembles in the domestic dark. She remembers how everyone in Natchez will suddenly grow quiet around her. Old Mrs. Marblehall, Mr. Marblehall's wife: she even goes out in the rain, which Southern women despise above everything, in big neat biscuit-colored galoshes, for which she "ordered off." She is only looking around — servile, undelighted, sleepy, expensive, tortured Mrs. Marblehall, pinning her mind with a pin to her husband's diet. She wants to tempt him, she tells him. What would he like best, that he can have?

There is Mr. Marblehall's ancestral home. It's not so wonderfully large — it has only four columns — but you always look toward it, the way you always glance into tunnels and see nothing. The river is after it now, and the little back garden has assuredly crumbled away, but the box maze is there on the edge like a trap, to confound the Mississippi River. Deep in the red wall waits the front door — it weighs such a lot, it is perfectly solid, all one piece, black mahogany. . . . And you see — one of *them* is always going in it. There is a knocker shaped like a gasping fish on the door. You have every reason in the world to imagine the inside is dark, with old things about. There's many a big, deathly looking tapestry, wrinkling and thin, many a sofa shaped like an S. Brocades as tall as the wicked queens in Italian tales stand gathered before the windows. Everything is draped and hooded and shaded, of course, unaffectionate but close. Such rosy lamps! The only sound would be a breath against the prisms, a stirring of the chandelier. It's like old eyelids, the house with one of its shutters, in careful working order, slowly opening outward. Then the little son softly comes and stares out like a kitten, with button nose and pointed ears and little fuzz of silky hair running along the top of his head.

The son is the worst of all. Mr. and Mrs. Marblehall had a child! When both of them were terribly old, they had this little, amazing, fascinating son. You can see how people are taken aback, how they jerk and throw up their hands every time they so much as think about it. At least, Mr. Marblehall sees them. He thinks Natchez people do nothing themselves, and really, most of them have done or could do the same thing. This son is six years old now. Close up, he has a monkey look, a very penetrating look. He has very sparse Japanese hair, tiny little pearly teeth, long little wilted fingers. Every day he is slowly and expensively dressed and taken to the Catholic school. He looks quietly and maliciously absurd, out walking with old Mr. Marblehall or old Mrs. Marblehall, placing his small booted foot on a little green worm, while they stop and wait on him. Everybody passing by thinks that he looks quite as if he thinks his parents had him just to show they could. You see, it becomes complicated, full of vindictiveness.

But now, as Mr. Marblehall walks as briskly as possible toward the river where there is sun, you have to merge him back into his proper blur, into the little party-giving town he lives in. Why look twice at him? There has been an old Mr. Marblehall in Natchez ever since the first one arrived back in 1818 — with a theatrical presentation of Otway's *Venice,* ending with *A Laughable Combat between Two Blind Fiddlers* — an actor! Mr. Marblehall isn't so important. His name is on the list, he is forgiven, but nobody gives a hoot about any old Mr. Marblehall. He could die, for all they care; some people even say, "Oh, is he still alive?" Mr. Marblehall walks and walks, and now and then he is driven in his ancient fringed carriage with the candle burners like empty eyes in front. And yes, he is supposed to travel for his health. But why consider his absence? There isn't any other place besides Natchez, and even if there were, it would hardly be likely to change Mr. Marblehall if it were brought up against him. Big fingers could pick him up off the Esplanade and take him through the air, his old legs still measuredly walking in a dangle, and set him down where he could continue that same old Natchez stroll of his in the East or the West or Kingdom Come. What difference could anything make now about old Mr. Marblehall — so late? A week or two would go by in Natchez and then there would be Mr. Marblehall, walking down Catherine Street again, still exactly in the same degree alive and old.

People naturally get bored. They say, "Well, he waited till he was sixty years old to marry, and what did he want to marry for?" as though what he did were the excuse for their boredom and their lack of concern. Even the thought of his having a stroke right in front of one of the Pilgrimage houses during Pilgrimage Week makes them only sigh, as if to say it's nobody's fault but his own if he wants to be so insultingly and precariously well-preserved. He ought to have a little black boy to follow around after him. Oh, his precious old health, which never had reason to be so inspiring! Mr. Marblehall has a formal, reproachful look as he stands on the corners arranging himself to go out into the traffic to cross the streets. It's as if he's thinking of shaking his stick and saying, "Well, look! I've done it, don't you see?" But really, nobody pays much attention to his look. He is just like other people to them. He could have easily danced with a troupe of angels in Paradise every night, and they wouldn't have guessed. Nobody is likely to find out that he is leading a double life.

The funny thing is he just recently began to lead this double life. He waited until he was sixty years old. Isn't he crazy? Before that, he'd never done anything. He didn't know what to do. Everything was for all the world like his first party. He stood about, and looked in his father's books, and long ago he went to France, but he didn't like it.

Drive out any of these streets in and under the hills and you find yourself lost. You see those scores of little galleried houses nearly alike. See the yellowing China trees at the eaves, the round flower beds in the front yards, like bites in the grass, listen to the screen doors whining, the ice wagons dragging by, the twittering noises of children. Nobody ever looks to see who is living in a house like that. These people come out themselves and sprinkle the hose over the street at this time of day to settle the dust, and after they sit on the porch, they go back into the house, and you hear the radio for the next two hours. It seems to mourn and cry for them. They go to bed early.

Well, old Mr. Marblehall can easily be seen standing beside a row of zinnias growing down the walk in front of that little house, bending over, easy, easy, so as not to strain anything, to stare at the flowers. Of course he planted them! They are covered with brown—each petal is a little heart-shaped pocket of dust. They don't have any smell, you know. It's twilight, all amplified with locusts screaming; nobody could see anything. Just what Mr. Marblehall is bending over the zinnias for is a mystery, any way you look at it. But there he is, quite visible, alive and old, leading his double life.

There's his other wife, standing on the night-stained porch by a potted fern, screaming things to a neighbor. This wife is really worse than the other one. She is more solid, fatter, shorter, and while not so ugly, funnier looking. She looks like funny furniture — an unornamented stairpost in one of these little houses, with her small monotonous round stupid head — or sometimes like a woodcut of a Bavarian witch, forefinger pointing, with scratches in the air all around her. But she's so static she scarcely moves, from her thick shoulders down past her cylindered brown dress to her short, stubby house slippers. She stands still and screams to the neighbors.

This wife thinks Mr. Marblehall's name is Mr. Bird. She says, "I declare I told Mr. Bird to go to bed, and look at him! I don't understand him!" All her devotion is combustible and goes up in despair. This wife tells everything she knows. Later, after she tells the neighbors, she will tell Mr. Marblehall. Cymbal-breasted, she fills the house with wifely complaints. She calls, "After I get Mr. Bird to bed, what does he do then? He lies there stretched out with his clothes on and don't have one word to say. Know what he does?"

And she goes on, while her husband bends over the zinnias, to tell what Mr. Marblehall (or Mr. Bird) does in bed. She does tell the truth. He reads *Terror Tales* and *Astonishing Stories*. She can't see anything to them: they scare her to death. These stories are about horrible and fantastic things happening to nude women and scientists. In one of them, when the characters open bureau drawers, they find a woman's leg with a stocking and garter on. Mrs. Bird had to shut the magazine. "The glutinous shadows," these stories say, "the red-eyed, muttering old crone," "the moonlight on her thigh," "an ancient cult of sun worshipers," "an altar suspiciously stained. . . ." Mr. Marblehall doesn't feel as terrified as all that, but he reads on and on. He is killing time. It is richness without taste, like some holiday food. The clock gets a fruity bursting tick, to get through midnight — then leisurely, leisurely on. When time is passing it's like a bug in his ear. And then Mr. Bird — he doesn't even want a shade on the light, this wife moans respectably. He reads under a bulb. She can tell you how he goes straight through a stack of magazines. "He might just as well not have a family," she always ends, unjustly, and rolls back into the house as if she had been on a little wheel all this time.

But the worst of them all is the other little boy. Another little boy just like the first one. He wanders around the bungalow full of tiny little schemes and jokes. He has lost his front tooth, and in this way he looks slightly different from Mr. Marblehall's other little boy — more shocking. Otherwise, you couldn't tell them apart if you wanted to. They both have that look of cunning little jugglers, violently small under some spotlight beam, preoccupied and silent, amusing themselves. Both of the children will go into sudden fits and tantrums that frighten their mothers and Mr. Marblehall to death. Then they can get anything they want. But this little boy, the one who's lost the tooth, is the smarter. For a long time he supposed that his mother was totally solid, down to her thick separated ankles. But when she stands there on the porch screaming to the neighbors, she reminds him of those flares that charm him so, that they leave burning in the street at night — the dark solid ball, then, tonguelike, the wicked, yellow, continuous, enslaving blaze on the stem. He knows what his father thinks.

Perhaps one day, while Mr. Marblehall is standing there gently bent over the zinnias, this little boy is going to write on a fence, "Papa leads a double life." He finds out things you wouldn't find out. He is a monkey.

You see, one night he is going to follow Mr. Marblehall (or Mr. Bird) out of the house. Mr. Marblehall has said as usual that he is leaving for one of his health trips. He is one of those correct old gentlemen who are still going to the wells and drinking the waters — exactly like his father, the late old Mr. Marblehall. But why does he leave on foot? This will occur to the little boy.

So he will follow his father. He will follow him all the way across town. He will see the shining river come winding around. He will see the house where Mr. Marblehall turns in at the wrought-iron gate. He will see a big speechless woman come out and lead him in by the heavy door. He will not miss those rosy lamps beyond the many-folded draperies at the windows. He will run around the fountains and around the japonica trees, past the stone figure of the pigtailed courtier mounted on the goat, down to the back of the house. From there he can look far up at the strange upstairs rooms. In one window the other wife will be standing like a giant, in a long-sleeved gathered nightgown, combing her electric hair and breaking it off each time in the comb. From the next window the other little boy will look out secretly into the night, and see him — or not see him. That would be an interesting thing, a moment of strange telepathies. (Mr. Marblehall can imagine it.) Then in the corner room there will suddenly be turned on the bright, naked light. Aha! Father!

Mr. Marblehall's little boy will easily climb a tree there and peep through the window. There, under a stark shadeless bulb, on a great four-poster with carved griffins, will be Mr. Marblehall, reading *Terror Tales,* stretched out and motionless.

Then everything will come out.

At first, nobody will believe it.

Or maybe the policeman will say, "Stop! How dare you!"

Maybe, better than that, Mr. Marblehall himself will confess his duplicity — how he has led two totally different lives, with completely different families, two sons instead of one. What an astonishing, unbelievable, electrifying confession that would be, and how his two wives would topple over, how his sons would cringe! To say nothing of most men aged sixty-six. So thinks self-consoling Mr. Marblehall.

You will think, what if nothing ever happens? What if there is no climax, even to this amazing life? Suppose old Mr. Marblehall simply remains alive, getting older by the minute, shuttling, still secretly, back and forth?

Nobody cares. Not an inhabitant of Natchez, Mississippi, cares if he is deceived by old Mr. Marblehall. Neither does anyone care that Mr. Marblehall has finally caught on, he thinks, to what people are supposed to do. This is it: they endure something inwardly — for a time secretly; they establish a past, a memory; thus they store up life. He has done this; most remarkably, he has even multiplied his life by deception; and plunging deeper and deeper he speculates upon some glorious finish, a great explosion of revelations . . . the future.

But he still has to kill time, and get through the clocking nights. Otherwise he dreams that he is a great blazing butterfly stitching up a net; which doesn't make sense.

Old Mr. Marblehall! He may have years ahead yet in which to wake up bolt upright in the bed under the naked bulb, his heart thumping, his old eyes watering and wild, imagining that if people knew about his double life, they'd die.